PLANNING
— and —
TEACHING
— in the —
STANDARDS-BASED
CLASSROOM

foreword by Robert J. Marzano

JEFF FLYGARE

JAN K. HOEGH

TAMMY HEFLEBOWER

MARZANO
Resources

555 North Morton Street
Bloomington, IN 47404
888.849.0851
FAX: 866.801.1447

email: info@MarzanoResources.com
MarzanoResources.com

Visit **MarzanoResources.com/reproducibles** to download the free reproducibles in this book.

Printed in the United States of America

Library of Congress Cataloging-in-Publication Data

Names: Flygare, Jeff, author. | Hoegh, Jan K., author. | Heflebower, Tammy,
   author.
Title: Planning and teaching in the standards-based classroom / Jeff
   Flygare, Tammy Heflebower, Jan K. Hoegh.
Description: Bloomington, IN : Solution Tree Press, 2021. | Includes
   bibliographical references and index.
Identifiers: LCCN 2021030204 (print) | LCCN 2021030205 (ebook) | ISBN
   9781943360710 (paperback) | ISBN 9781943360727 (ebook)
Subjects: LCSH: Education--Standards--United States. | Lesson
   planning--United States.
Classification: LCC LB3060.83 .F59 2021 (print) | LCC LB3060.83 (ebook) |
   DDC 379.73--dc23
LC record available at https://lccn.loc.gov/2021030204
LC ebook record available at https://lccn.loc.gov/2021030205

Production Team
President and Publisher: Douglas M. Rife
Associate Publisher: Sarah Payne-Mills
Managing Production Editor: Kendra Slayton
Editorial Director: Todd Brakke
Art Director: Rian Anderson
Copy Chief: Jessi Finn
Senior Production Editor: Laurel Hecker
Content Development Specialist: Amy Rubenstein
Copy Editor: Mark Hain
Proofreader: Sarah Ludwig
Text and Cover Designer: Kelsey Hergül
Editorial Assistants: Sarah Ludwig and Elijah Oates

Acknowledgments

Marzano Resources would like to thank the following reviewers:

Tonya Alexander
English Teacher (NBCT)
Owego Free Academy
Owego, New York

Kimberly Freiley
ELA Teacher
Ingersoll Middle School
Canton, Illinois

Jennifer LaBollita
Assistant Director, Office of Multilingual
    Education
Framingham Public Schools
Framingham, Massachusetts

Lauren Smith
Instructional Coach
Noble Crossing Elementary School
Noblesville, Indiana

Table of Contents

About the Authors

Jeff Flygare is a former classroom teacher, English department chair, professional developer, and building leader. During his twenty-six-year career teaching middle school drama and high school English in Academy District 20 in Colorado, he taught nearly every course in his school's English department. Jeff developed classes in mythology, Shakespeare, philosophy, and comparative religions, and worked with social studies colleagues to create an interdisciplinary class called World Studies, which he team-taught successfully for seventeen years. He taught Advanced Placement (AP) English classes for twenty-one years and served as an AP English literature reader and table leader for Educational Testing Service for many years. He adopted standards-based learning in his classroom and successfully taught students at all levels in a standards-based environment for many years.

Jeff also has a strong theatrical background, working first as an actor and then as a director at a major regional theater company in Colorado. He directed many high school productions, both traditional and Shakespearean, as well. As a Marzano Resources associate, Jeff travels around the world to work with educators on topics involving curriculum, instruction, and assessment. He is the author of *Close Reading in the Secondary Classroom* and coauthor of *A Teacher's Guide to Standards-Based Learning*.

Jeff holds a bachelor's degree in English from the State University of New York at Buffalo, a master's degree in English from the University of Colorado Denver, and a master's degree in education with an endorsement in gifted education from the University of Colorado Colorado Springs.

Jan K. Hoegh has been an educator for over thirty years and an author and associate for Marzano Resources since 2010. Prior to joining the Marzano team, she was a classroom teacher, building leader, professional development specialist, high school assistant principal, curriculum coordinator, and assistant director of statewide assessment for the Nebraska Department of Education, where her primary focus was Nebraska State Accountability test development. Jan has served on a variety of statewide and national standards and assessment committees and has presented at numerous conferences around the world.

As an associate with Marzano Resources, Jan works with educators across the United States and beyond as they strive to improve student achievement. Her passion for education, combined with extensive knowledge of curriculum, instruction, and assessment, provide credible support for teachers, leaders, schools, and districts. High-quality classroom assessment and grading practices are her primary training focuses. She is the author of *A Handbook for Developing and Using Proficiency Scales in the Classroom* and coauthor of *Collaborative Teams That Transform Schools*, *A School Leader's Guide to Standards-Based Grading*, and *A Teacher's Guide to Standards-Based Learning*, as well as other publications.

Jan holds a bachelor's degree in elementary education and a master of arts in educational administration, both from the University of Nebraska at Kearney. She also earned a specialization in assessment from the University of Nebraska–Lincoln.

 **Tammy Heflebower, EdD,** is a highly sought-after school leader and consultant with vast experiences in urban, rural, and suburban districts throughout the United States, Australia, Canada, Denmark, Great Britain, and the Netherlands. She has served as an award-winning classroom teacher, building leader, district leader, regional professional development director, and national and international trainer. She has also been an adjunct professor of curriculum, instruction, and assessment at several universities, and a prominent member and leader of numerous statewide and national educational organizations.

She was vice president and then senior scholar at Marzano Resources and continues to work as an author and associate with Marzano Resources and Solution Tree. In addition, Tammy is the CEO of her own company, !nspire Inc.: Education and Business Solutions, specializing in powerful presentation and facilitation techniques, which she writes about and shares worldwide. Tammy is sole author of the *Presenting Perfected* book series and lead author of *Crafting Your Message: Tips and Tricks for Educators to Deliver Perfect Presentations*. She is also lead author of the best-selling and award-winning *A School Leader's Guide to Standards-Based Grading*, lead author of the award-finalist *A Teacher's Guide to Standards-Based Learning*, and coauthor of *Collaborative Teams That Transform Schools: The Next Step in PLCs* and *Teaching and Assessing 21st Century Skills*. She is a contributing author to over a dozen other books and publications, many of which have been translated into multiple languages and are referenced internationally.

Tammy holds a bachelor's degree from Hastings College, where she was honored as Outstanding Young Alumna and her volleyball team was inducted into the athletic hall of fame. She has a master of arts from the University of Nebraska Omaha, and she received her educational administrative endorsement and doctorate from the University of Nebraska–Lincoln.

To book Jeff Flygare, Jan K. Hoegh, or Tammy Heflebower for professional development, contact pd@MarzanoResources.com.

Foreword

By Robert J. Marzano

This book is about building a bridge to the future. Whether it's obvious or not, the K–12 system of schooling in the United States is in the midst of a massage shift in how it goes about the business of educating our young people. The shift is from a system designed to matriculate students through an established curriculum in age-based groups to a system designed to allow individual students to move at their own pace through the established curriculum. In the current age-based system, all students of a given age receive the same content—students who are at the chronological age to be classified as fourth graders receive the fourth-grade curriculum in all subject areas regardless of their knowledge and skill in each subject area. Students who are at the chronological age to be classified as eighth graders receive the eighth-grade curriculum in all subject areas regardless of their knowledge and skill in a given subject area, and so on. In the system of the future, the process of moving through a school's curriculum will be quite different. Students who would chronologically be classified as fourth graders but have the knowledge and skill to work on seventh-grade mathematics will, in fact, work on seventh-grade mathematics. Students who would be chronologically classified as eighth graders but are capable of learning advanced high school mathematics will, in fact, study advanced high school mathematics, and so on. At a personal level, I believe this future is inevitable. The only question regarding that future is how quickly it will manifest.

Even though this future system seems intuitively appealing and needed, it requires massive structural transformations, not the least of which involve changing grading policies and scheduling policies. In effect, for a school to manifest the new, competency-based future, it must change practices that have been in place for so many decades that their inertia makes them formidable (albeit not insurmountable) obstacles. To overcome such obstacles takes detailed planning; a gradual process of implementation; education for parents, guardians, students, and the community at large; and, above all, time. These daunting facts have lead some schools to simply file their dreams of a brighter future on a shelf, to be dusted off and examined at some later time. Fortunately, with this book, Jeff Flygare, Jan K. Hoegh, and Tammy Heflebower provide a starting place that schools at all levels might employ to begin their journey without drastically changing their status quo. In effect, this book represents a bridge to a competency-based future. The foundation of that bridge is the use of proficiency scales as organizers for standards-based curriculum, instruction, and assessment. I have found that once schools begin employing proficiency scales, they start to see the possibility of a competency-based future and, in turn, start making plans to manifest it.

I have developed and utilized proficiency scales since the early 1990s. Since their conception, proficiency scales have become a staple for organizing curriculum, instruction, and assessments for teachers in every state. In this book, Flygare, Hoegh, and Heflebower demonstrate how proficiency scales can be generated from priority standards, how they can be used to set goals for student learning, and how they can be used to design assessments. The authors also add an new level of clarity to the use of proficiency scales with their eight-step instructional cycle. This can be applied to any subject area, at any grade level, in any type of system. Finally, this book demonstrates how proficiency scales can be a quintessential tool in communicating students' status and growth to all interested constituents.

For those looking to take the first step toward competency-based education, this is the book to read.

Robert J. Marzano
Chief Academic Officer
Marzano Resources

Introduction

It used to be simple.

Content was what educators had to teach each year. Understanding of that content informed decisions about how teachers sequenced instruction. Long years of experience and teachers' own intuition about what students needed served them well. Students learned through tried and true instructional strategies. From the teachers' perspective, students seemed interested and asked questions, and teachers could see learning happen.

Then the standards movement emerged, and it didn't much affect what teachers did. Standardized tests were aligned to the standards, and teachers were tasked with making sure that they were aligning their teaching to those same standards. A quick look at the standards suggested that existing instruction aligned rather well. Most teachers felt they were meeting the requirements. But sometimes the tests suggested otherwise. Though concerning, the problem didn't merit much change in what educators were doing. After all, teachers could see the learning happening.

But education was changing in a fundamental way. Throughout the world, the move to outcomes-based education meant new challenges for educators. In the United States, education fundamentally changed in 2002 when Congress passed and President George W. Bush signed into law the Elementary and Secondary Education Act, more commonly known as No Child Left Behind (NCLB, 2002). The most visible changes were state tests, standards, and accountability. But the underlying change was more profound. Before NCLB, the job of educators was to offer learning and to identify those who learned and those who did not. After NCLB, teachers had to find ways to ensure *every* student learned. That is a very different and much more difficult task. It is also a task shared by educators all over the world. Countries as diverse as Canada, India, Russia, and Turkey have adopted the basic principles of outcome-based education. In Canada, while there is no federal-level education ministry, each provincial or territorial government upholds educational standards and benchmarks. Identifying the educational goals for students and holding them accountable for that learning is familiar territory in Canadian schools (National Center on Education and the Economy, n.d.).

In this new world, strategies and teaching methods educators had used for years needed to be revised. Educators' thinking about learning had to undergo a change, too. It was no longer enough to present content; standards defined clear end goals that all students now needed to reach. Throughout instruction, teachers had to monitor all students' learning and adjust instruction to make sure each student was making progress. Thus, planning and instruction became much more complicated.

But no one told teachers how to do that planning and instructing. Somehow, they were just supposed to do it.

That problem is the genesis of this book. As much as standards have been at the forefront of discussions about education for the first two decades of the 21st century, classroom teachers are still hindered by a deficit of guidance for teaching students to achieve those standards. In this book, we offer practical advice about how classroom teachers can adjust the processes of planning and instruction to align with essential standards, including making sure that selected instructional strategies help students develop the specific knowledge and skills required by the standards. For each activity, assignment, or assessment, we provide advice for ensuring that students benefit in specific ways that are related to the standards identified for the grade level or course.

Whether you are new to the profession or a veteran of decades, you will find useful information and processes related to standards-based planning, instruction, assessment, and feedback. The planning and teaching processes we describe are compatible with virtually any instructional model used by schools or districts, as well as with traditional, standards-based, and standards-referenced grading and reporting methods.

Standards and Content

In the fundamental shift to standards-based learning, many educators encounter what appears to be a dichotomy between content versus standards. In a traditional, content-based approach, teachers often begin with a resource like a textbook or a curriculum guide that sequences specific content and design instruction to work through that content sequence. The curriculum often becomes, from the students' point of view, a series of facts and bits of information that are sometimes unrelated. Teachers and students may see the purpose of instruction as working through a body of information or skills, unrelated to anything but itself.

By contrast, a standards-based approach means that teachers begin with the identified educational standards for a particular course or grade level. Then, teachers sequence the development of the knowledge and skills required by these standards and design instruction along specific lines that foster that development. Resources such as textbooks are used to aid that development, but they no longer are the primary organizing force of the curriculum.

Teachers who shift to standards-based instruction may find focusing on standards instead of content to be difficult. After all, you may have taught your content for years, you are familiar with it, and standards are relatively new. The good news is that your content will still be there, just in a slightly different context. Your years of experience will serve you well as you see the content in a new way. New teachers may find this shift in focus challenging as well. It could be that you entered the profession of teaching because of your deep love of a particular content area, and you are enthusiastic to share that love with your students. Be assured that you will be able to do so—within the context of developing knowledge and skills as defined by the standards. In the end, it isn't a choice between standards or content at all. The standards provide a logical sequencing of learning, and essential content will fit within that sequence. But the thought processes involved in standards-based planning and instruction represent a paradigm shift for most educators.

For example, an English language arts (ELA) teacher may continue to share the same beloved works of literature with students as he has in the past. However, he now does so to help students master standards related to literary devices rather than simply because the books are part of the so-called canon. A social studies teacher might still arrange instructional units in chronological order, but the goal of each unit is student proficiency with the relevant social themes and civic concepts rather than the simple memorization of historical events. A science teacher can still employ her favorite demonstrations of chemical reactions, but with an eye toward imparting skills that are applicable across multiple concepts in chemistry, or indeed across multiple scientific disciplines.

This paradigm shift will affect students as well. State or provincial standards are the focus of school and district accountability, and teachers are held responsible for student progress on these standards. In schools and districts where standards are the foundation of learning, students will be aware of the standards and will want to understand their own progress on them. Early in the learning process, the teacher will share the standards with students, identify examples of student performance at various levels of proficiency on the standards, help students understand the sequence of learning they will encounter, and make the standards a central point of everything done in the classroom. These standards-based practices show students the relevance of the activities, assignments, and assessments done in class. Clear purpose helps students encounter learning with a positive attitude. Shifting your focus to a standards-based approach may be intimidating, but it is important and will benefit both you and your students.

An Overview of Standards-Based Learning

The standards-based approach influences every aspect of classroom practice, from curriculum to unit planning to lesson delivery to assessment to grading. This all-encompassing nature is why we refer to this system as *standards-based learning* (as opposed to other common terms like *standards-based grading*). Standards are the foundation of the system, but educators will transform and apply those standards in various ways to effectively support student learning.

A standards-based curriculum is not merely a list of standards. Most sets of course or grade-level standards contain far too much information for teachers to reasonably cover in the instructional time available. Thus, educators must prioritize standards to create a *guaranteed and viable curriculum* (Marzano, Warrick, & Simms, 2014). *Guaranteed* means that teachers who teach the same grade level or course use and teach the same priority standards, eliminating variability in what students learn when assigned to different classes. *Viable* means that the amount of material covered is reasonable, so teachers can provide effective instruction and ensure student learning within the allotted instructional time rather than rush to cover too many topics.

To make the standards more functional for instruction, educators can craft *learning progressions* that define basic, target, and advanced levels of a standard or a closely related group of standards. The format we recommend is the *proficiency scale* developed by education researcher Robert J. Marzano (2006, 2009), shown in figure I.1. When creating a proficiency scale, an educator uses the standard as a starting point to write learning targets for each level of the scale. These learning targets represent three levels: content that is simpler and therefore a prerequisite to reaching proficiency on the standard, content at the level of the standard, and more complex content that is beyond the standard. These learning progressions scaffold student learning and guide teachers' unit and lesson planning. In fact, proficiency scales become a central tool of instruction, assessment, and feedback, with lessons, test questions, and scores all based on the scale. Because the scales are an augmentation of the standards themselves, lessons, test items, and scores related to scales are also standards based.

Score	Description
4.0	Advanced content
3.0	Target content
2.0	Simpler content necessary for proficiency
1.0	With help, partial success with score 2.0 content and score 3.0 content
0.0	Even with help, no success

Figure I.1: Generic form of a proficiency scale.

Teachers can use proficiency scales to plan units and individual lessons, including instruction on basic and target content, practice with this content, and opportunities for going beyond mastery. Assessments are also a key part of this plan. Aligning assessment tasks to scales and scoring responses accordingly tells teachers and students exactly what students know and can do with respect to the standards. For example, if a teacher develops test questions based on the score 2.0 learning target from the proficiency scale, a student who regularly answers all those questions correctly clearly understands the simpler content. Checking in on students' progress in this way and analyzing assessment data throughout the unit (that is, formative assessment) allows teachers to adjust instruction accordingly and provide support for all learners. This process of planning, teaching, assessing, and adjusting is what we call the *instructional cycle*.

With this overview in mind, the following sections highlight the changes that occur with this paradigm shift to standards-based learning and the benefits that result.

Changes to the Planning and Teaching Process

For educators who have spent years teaching more traditionally by developing students' understanding of a body of content, using standards may represent a substantial change in the planning and teaching process. To reiterate, instructional planning in a standards-based system begins with a selection of important standards rather than content. For example, a ninth-grade ELA teacher might teach the interpretation of reading, specifically in dramatic form, as represented in the following Common Core State Standards.

- Analyze how complex characters (e.g., those with multiple or conflicting motivations) develop over the course of a text, interact with other characters, and advance the plot or develop the theme (RL.9–10.3; National Governors Association Center for Best Practices [NGA] & Council of Chief State School Officers [CCSSO], 2010a).

- By the end of grade 9, read and comprehend literature, including stories, dramas, and poems, in the grades 9–10 text complexity band proficiently, with scaffolding as needed at the high end of the range (RL.9–10.10; NGA & CCSSO, 2010a).

These standards represent what a teacher or team of teachers decides is essential in the learning students will do over the instructional cycle. A typical text that is taught in ninth grade, Shakespeare's *Romeo and Juliet*, would represent content that supports the teaching of these two standards. Note however, that in developing a unit plan, the teacher identifies the standards to work on and then identifies the supporting text, rather than the other way around as in a traditional content-based approach.

By beginning with the identified standards, teachers can gradually scaffold learning of the standards through properly sequencing not only the content but also instructional strategies. In the example of a ninth-grade ELA unit involving *Romeo and Juliet*, the teacher would identify simpler content and skills that would be taught early in the instructional cycle and scaffold the learning toward proficiency in the two identified standards, as follows.

- Analyze how complex characters (e.g., those with multiple or conflicting motivations) develop over the course of a text, interact with other characters, and advance the plot or develop the theme (RL.9–10.3; NGA & CCSSO, 2010a).

  Simpler knowledge and skills: Identify major and minor characters, identify motivations of specific characters, identify plot elements, identify themes in a large work

- By the end of grade 9, read and comprehend literature, including stories, dramas, and poems, in the grades 9–10 text complexity band proficiently, with scaffolding as needed at the high end of the range (RL.9–10.10; NGA & CCSSO, 2010a).

  Simpler knowledge and skills: Read and understand poetry, identify the basic elements of Shakespearean style

Once the teachers or teams identify these elements, they can arrange them in a learning progression using a proficiency scale and then identify or design appropriate instructional strategies and activities to scaffold the learning through the instructional cycle.

Teachers can also plan to carefully monitor student progress throughout the learning period with frequent classroom assessments that are aligned to the standards. In the case of this example, teachers would want to craft assessments that measure student ability to identify major and minor characters in the text as well as character motivations. Knowing those abilities are solid would ensure much higher student achievement when students move to level 3.0, the level of proficiency on the standards themselves. At level 3.0, students would be assessed on their ability to discuss the development of characters over the course of the text. Using the data from these assessments in a formative manner, teachers can adjust the instructional plan during the unit, thereby meeting students' learning needs as they develop proficiency on the standards. By the end of the learning period, teachers will know exactly where students are on the learning progression of the priority standards. When state testing arrives, there will be no surprises; performance on the state tests will mirror that of students in the classroom (Haystead, 2016).

As mentioned previously, standards establish the learning goals for students, and it is the teacher's responsibility to help *all* students meet those goals. It is quite likely that every classroom will have students with varying degrees of ability to learn the content. For example, some students will be reading grade-appropriate texts independently, others will have the ability to read texts above grade level, and a certain number of students will likely be reading below grade level. These different ability levels can present challenges to any classroom teacher when it comes to ensuring students master the knowledge and skills of grade-level or course standards. For some students, these variations may categorize them as *exceptional learners*. These include students with disabilities, English learners, and gifted and talented students (Heflebower, Hoegh, & Warrick, 2014). We propose that the term *exceptional learners* also refers to *any* student who needs special attention in order to learn the academic content presented in the standards-based classroom. Teachers must plan to support these learners as a regular part of the instructional cycle.

Fortunately, standards-based learning provides the opportunity and framework to easily identify and meet the needs of every student in your classroom. By using proficiency scales and their clear learning progression to measure student progress, teachers will understand students' learning needs at each level of the scale. This approach ensures educational equity by addressing the specific needs of each student in the class.

Benefits You Can Expect

Why change to standards-based planning and instruction? For some teachers, this may be a decision handed down from above and they may have little choice. Many school districts are switching to standards-based instruction as a method to ensure learning for every student. Some teachers may have personally chosen to adopt a standards-based approach for their classrooms without a districtwide or schoolwide mandate. Regardless of the impetus, standards-based learning has numerous benefits, including the following (Alsalhi, Eltahir, & Al-Qatawneh, 2019; Heinrich, Darling-Aduana, Good, & Cheng, 2019; Iamarino, 2014; Palloff & Pratt, 2007).

- Clear and concise learning goals
- Clarity of expectations for proficiency

1

Curriculum Based on Standards and Scales

The foundation of a standards-based approach is, of course, standards. Before standards-based planning and instruction can occur, educators must analyze the standards and transform them into a guaranteed and viable curriculum. These phases of implementation often occur at the school or district level rather than in individual classrooms. However, for the purpose of background knowledge, we review the processes of prioritizing standards and developing proficiency scales in this chapter. For more detail, please consult *A School Leader's Guide to Standards-Based Grading* (Heflebower et al., 2014) and *A Handbook for Developing and Using Proficiency Scales in the Classroom* (Hoegh, 2020).

Priority Standards

The first step in creating a standards-based learning system is to distill the relevant standards into a manageable set of content. Teachers are expected to teach a vast array of state or provincial standards. Yet teachers quickly discern that not all these standards are of equal importance. In fact, some are even quite repetitive. Analyses have revealed that many standards documents available for schools and districts articulate more content than is possible to teach practically in the time available to teachers—even after updates intended to address this concern (Marzano, 2003; Marzano & Yanoski, 2016; Marzano, Yanoski, Hoegh, & Simms, 2013; Porter, McMaken, Hwang, & Yang, 2011). In almost all cases, it would be impossible for a teacher to teach every single standard set forth for his or her content area and grade level. Therefore, teachers must determine which standards are most important—that is, which are *priority standards*—to create a viable, focused set of standards for each content area, course, or grade level. We refer to the remaining standards not determined to be a priority as *supporting standards* (Heflebower, Hoegh, Warrick, & Flygare, 2019). Students will still learn the supporting standards, but they will not be the main focus of units or assessments. In the following sections, we explore the process and the qualities by which teachers prioritize standards, and then discuss particular considerations for doing this work as a team or independently.

Understanding the Process and Criteria

Fundamentally, creating a set of priority standards involves (1) appraising each standard against several criteria and (2) comparing the appraisals to determine which standards are most important.

Education consultant and author Larry Ainsworth (2003) suggested three common criteria for assessing standards.

1. **Endurance:** Knowledge and skills that will last beyond a class period or course

2. **Leverage:** Knowledge and skills that cross over into many domains of learning

3. **Readiness:** Knowledge and skills important to subsequent content or courses

Our experience has indicated that teachers should also consider two additional criteria.

4. **Assessment:** Knowledge and skills that will appear on high-stakes assessments

5. **Teacher judgment:** A professional's expert opinion on which knowledge and skills are more or less important for students to master

For each standard, think critically about each of the five criteria and make a judgment about whether or not the standard meets each criterion. Don't overthink it: your first inclination is sufficient at this stage. There is a delicate balance between speed and accuracy. You certainly want to reflect thoughtfully about each standard but not get too bogged down in the process. As an example of how a hypothetical team of teachers might evaluate a specific standard for these five criteria, consider the following Canadian grade 4 mathematics standard.

> Whole Numbers (B1.1): By the end of Grade 4, students will read, represent, compose, and decompose whole numbers up to and including 10,000, using appropriate tools and strategies, and describe various ways they are used in everyday life. (Queen's Printer for Ontario, n.d.a)

This provincial standard demonstrates endurance, because students will use these skills long after the test; leverage, in that these skills are applicable in multiple disciplines (mathematics and science); and readiness, since they are transferable to later content areas or courses. Because the skills listed in this standard would be required on many standardized tests, this standard also meets the assessment criterion. The experienced teachers on the team evaluating the standard find it to be very valuable, because students will need to read, represent, compose, and decompose numbers in various life settings (budgets, financial plans, and so on), so it meets the teacher judgment criterion as well. When a standard meets most or all of the five criteria, as in this example, it is most often deemed a priority standard.

In contrast, consider the elementary social-emotional learning (SEL) skill "Develop self-awareness and sense of identity" (Queen's Printer for Ontario, n.d.c). While this standard may have some measure of endurance and leverage, it contains fewer readiness skills than the first standard. Because self-awareness and sense of identity most likely do not appear on a district or provincial assessment, this standard does not meet the assessment criterion. Regarding teacher judgment, the teachers reviewing this standard indicate that this standard is important, but should be a supporting standard that is taught in concert with other character-related curriculum. They might suggest that they will use various content areas to model and monitor a student's self-awareness and sense of identity. Therefore, the teacher team might decide to make the whole-numbers standard a priority standard but not the SEL skill standard. Figure 1.1 shows how teachers might record their evaluations of specific standards.

Standards	Endurance	Leverage	Readiness	Assessment	Teacher Judgment
By the end of Grade 4, students will read, represent, compose, and decompose whole numbers up to and including 10,000, using appropriate tools and strategies, and describe various ways they are used in everyday life (B1.1)	✓	✓	✓	✓	✓
Develop self-awareness and sense of identity	✓	✓			

Source: Adapted from Heflebower et al., 2014.

Source for standards: Queen's Printer for Ontario, n.d.a, n.d.c.

Figure 1.1: Priority standards decision matrix.

After using specific criteria such as endurance, leverage, readiness, assessment, and teacher judgment to assess each of the standards for a specific content area, course, or grade level, the next step is to compare the results. Those standards that have check marks across all five criteria naturally surface as priority standards; in figure 1.1, the whole-numbers standard is therefore a priority standard. Those that only have one or two checks are more likely going to become supporting standards; in figure 1.1, the self-awareness standard represents a supporting standard. A *supporting* designation does not imply that these standards are not important or will not be taught. Most likely, teachers will spend less instructional time on supporting standards compared to priority standards and would assess them alongside priority standards rather than dedicating a separate assessment to them. The goal is to have a comprehensive list of twelve to fifteen priority standards per course or grade level and content area. There may be many additional supporting standards that find their place as secondary learning targets.

It is best if teachers complete the prioritization work within one full-day session lasting five to six hours. The reason is that it is difficult to recall the essence of the discussions if days or weeks pass. If, however, a single session is not possible, then consider shorter sessions scheduled closer together. This way, teachers spend less time rehashing previous discussions and can more efficiently complete this part of the process.

Over years of working with teachers on identifying priority and supporting standards, we have noted challenges in some particular subjects. Additional considerations arise especially for noncore content areas (those beyond the core academic subjects). If you work in disciplines such as career and technical education (CTE), fine arts, or performing arts, your standards may be organized into grade bands instead of individual grade levels. The same standards-prioritization process works for grade-band standards as for grade-level standards, but the challenge is that you must first determine which standards best fit particular grade levels or courses. So, there is an additional step: look at the grade bands, determine which standards will be in which grade levels or courses, and then move to the prioritization process.

CTE teachers have academic standards, but they are also charged—to a much more substantial degree than most other teachers—to develop the skills that turn students into good employees. CTE teachers should consider the importance of career-readiness standards and include them in the prioritization process. For example, take this secondary CTE standard from Nevada: "Demonstrate understanding of workplace organizations, systems, and climates by identifying 'big picture' issues and fulfilling the mission of the workplace" (Nevada Department of Education, 2014). Employability skills are important content in CTE and are likely candidates for priority standards.

A similar situation emerges in the performing arts regarding those skills that make for strong performances in courses like chorus, band, and drama. For instance, take this drama and theater arts standard for seventh grade in Colorado: "Select, analyze and interpret artistic work for presentation" (Colorado Department of Education, 2020). Due to the nature of the performance content, such skills often surface as priority standards within such disciplines.

Prioritizing Standards With a School or District Team

As mentioned previously, standards prioritization often takes place at the school or district level. If you are a teacher in a school or district that is (or soon will be) in the process of moving to standards-based learning, consider getting directly involved by serving on the design team for your content area or grade level. Often there will be a request for assistance from your district curriculum office. Your principal is likely to seek interest at the building level. In some cases, getting involved may be as simple as volunteering. In other cases, particularly if you are in a very large district, there may be an application form to complete. This is to help ensure representation from various grade levels and courses, as well as to clearly articulate the nature of the work. If you are an elementary teacher, you would likely work on a grade-level team for multiple content areas, as most elementary teachers are generalists. If you are a secondary teacher and more likely to teach just one or two content areas, you will have direct input into identifying the priority standards for these particular content areas. In either case, you will have a voice in what is emphasized across the school or district.

Serving on a school or district design team will likely take some time out of your classroom or summer and require trying new things in your classroom, but it will be well worth the standards and assessment literacy you gain as a professional. You will make initial decisions about which standards are most essential for students by assessing each one against the five aforementioned criteria and discussing the results with your colleagues. After completing an initial draft of priority standards, as a design team participant, you will pilot the use of priority standards in your classroom and begin to align them to your curriculum resources. Additionally, you may be tasked with obtaining and reviewing feedback from colleagues not serving on the design team about the prioritization work. In some cases, this may be done through a survey instrument; in others, it may mean you are tasked with taking the draft version of the priority standards back to a meeting with your site, content-area, or grade-level teams for review, discussion, and feedback. Afterward, you will bring your colleagues' feedback back to the design team to incorporate or refute.

Prioritizing Standards Independently

If your school or district is not shifting to standards-based learning, you can do so independently. We must mention that this method of prioritizing standards is the least recommended, as it perpetuates variation in what students assigned to different classrooms learn. If standards are prioritized separately teacher by teacher, building by building, a pervasive lack of consistency occurs. However, if you are ready to move to standards-based learning but your district and your building are not, then this may be your only option.

Follow the same process as outlined previously (page 12) to evaluate each standard according to the priority criteria. However, since you do not have colleagues to discuss results with, you will now want to check your thinking with an outside source. For example, you could look at the websites of districts that post their priority standards online. Many districts do this, including the City of Saint Charles School District in Missouri (www.stcharlessd.org), Wichita Public Schools in Kansas (www.usd259.org), and Rutland City Public Schools in Vermont (www.rutlandcitypublicschools.org). Another comprehensive set for comparison is the Critical Concepts produced by Marzano Resources (n.d.a). The Critical Concepts include lists of essential topics for English language arts, mathematics, science, and social studies.

Once you have identified priority and supporting standards, the next step is to create the documents that will guide your use of those standards through every step of the learning ahead—high-quality proficiency scales. That is the subject of the next section.

Proficiency Scales

Proficiency scales are the way that priority standards come to life in a classroom—for teachers, students, and parents. Scales allow users to see, in detail, the specific knowledge and skills that must be mastered at varying levels of proficiency. The scale is a clear road map for all. As a teacher, you need a thorough understanding of the concept of proficiency scales and how they are developed, as you will use them for all the rest of the standards-based learning processes and products.

Understanding Proficiency Scales

In essence, a proficiency scale defines a learning progression for a specific topic, which is often defined by a given priority standard. The scale demonstrates for both teachers and students what proficiency looks like, what knowledge and skills are needed to achieve proficiency, and how students might go beyond proficiency within a specific priority standard (Heflebower et al., 2019). Figure 1.2 shows the generic form of a proficiency scale.

Score	Description
4.0	Advanced content
3.0	Target content
2.0	Simpler content necessary for proficiency
1.0	With help, partial success with score 2.0 content and score 3.0 content
0.0	Even with help, no success

Figure 1.2: Generic form of a proficiency scale.

As you see on this generic version, score 3.0 is the heart of the proficiency scale; it defines the target content and skills that teachers expect all students to know and be able to do. When creating a proficiency scale, teachers place the wording of a standard or other statement of expectations at score 3.0. Score 2.0 describes the simpler content—the foundational knowledge and skills that students will need to master before progressing to proficiency. This often includes vocabulary and basic facts. Score 4.0 provides students the opportunity to go above and beyond expectations by applying their knowledge in new situations or demonstrating understanding beyond what the teacher directly teaches in class. We refer to the specific content at each level of the scale as *learning targets*, because each item of content (or related set of items) will be the goal for a lesson or series of lessons. Students must master the learning targets for each level, typically before moving onto the next level. These learning targets form the basis of your lessons within your instructional cycles.

A question many educators have when they encounter proficiency scales for the first time is whether a proficiency scale is a rubric, a device most teachers have used for many years. While there are many similarities, there are important differences between the two devices. Proficiency scales and rubrics both identify different levels of student performance and can be used to evaluate student performance. One important difference is that a rubric is usually written to evaluate student performance on a specific task or assignment, while a proficiency scale is created to describe a learning progression on a set of learning targets related to a priority standard. Therefore, a proficiency scale, unlike a rubric, is used throughout the learning cycle; indeed, it may be used across learning cycles, while a rubric is used for a specific activity or assignment. Another important distinction between the two is that while a proficiency scale helps to define a guaranteed and viable curriculum by incorporating essential content that will be taught and assessed, a rubric may contain content that is important (for example, conventions in writing) but not directly related to the learning progression on a priority standard.

A proficiency scale must be *unidimensional*—that is, focused on one element of target content at score 3.0. If a scale contains multiple score 3.0 learning targets, those elements must covary. *Covariance* simply means that as a student's knowledge or skill in one element increases, his or her knowledge or skill in the other element also increases because the elements are closely related (Marzano, 2018). Applying the concept of covariance to a proficiency scale means that the content within a scale is narrowly focused and closely related. The scale covers a specific topic and does not include tangential material.

Score 2.0 content supports students' progression toward proficiency on the topic defined at score 3.0. The content at this level is aligned to the score 3.0 learning targets, and guides students to learn basic knowledge and skills that prepare them for the target content. Score 1.0 and score 0.0 of the proficiency scale do not involve specific content. Rather, score 1.0 indicates that a student can demonstrate some knowledge or skill with significant help from the teacher, but not independently. Score 0.0 means that even with help a student cannot show any understanding.

Figure 1.3 depicts a sample proficiency scale as a teacher might use it in a classroom, with specific topical and grade-level content, in this case for a fifth-grade physical science class. The scale in figure 1.3 defines the learning progression for the fifth-grade science topic of material properties. Score 3.0 describes the learning target that all students must reach, score 2.0 describes foundational vocabulary and processes, and score 4.0 describes an advanced task, which would demonstrate a student's ability to go beyond proficiency expectations.

Score 4.0	The student will solve an engineering problem involving decisions about which material, based on its properties, will best satisfy a set of requirements and constraints.
Score 3.5	In addition to score 3.0 performance, partial success at score 4.0 content
Score 3.0	The student will classify materials based on their properties (magnetism, conductivity, density, solubility, boiling point, melting point).
Score 2.5	No major errors or omissions regarding score 2.0 content, and partial success at score 3.0 content
Score 2.0	Student will recognize and recall basic vocabulary, such as *magnetism*, *conductivity*, *density*, *solubility*, *boiling point*, and *melting point*. Student will perform basic processes, such as: • Making observations to identify the properties of a material • Taking measurements to identify the properties of a material
Score 1.5	Partial success at score 2.0 content, and major errors or omissions regarding score 3.0 content
Score 1.0	With help, the student will achieve partial success at score 2.0 content and score 3.0 content.
Score 0.5	With help, partial success at score 2.0 content but not at score 3.0 content
Score 0.0	Even with help, the student has no success.

Source: Adapted from Marzano, Norford, Finn, & Finn, 2017.

Figure 1.3: Proficiency scale for a fifth-grade science topic.

Figure 1.4 is a high school social studies example for the following priority standard: "Students will analyze how major past and current events are chronologically connected and evaluate their impact on one another" (California Department of Education, 2020). In this example, the teacher elected to break the standard statement into bulleted learning targets. This way, it is more clearly delineated, and signifies how specific lessons will address specific learning targets.

Score 4.0	In addition to score 3.0, in-depth inferences and applications that go beyond what was taught. *Identify two events from the same time period that had significant impact. Identify which event had more impact and provide evidence to support the decision.*
Score 3.5	In addition to score 3.0 performance, partial success at score 4.0 content
Score 3.0	The student will: • *Relate past and present events to one another* • *Critique the effects of past and present events* • *Predict plausible future outcomes based on past events* The student exhibits no major errors or omissions.
Score 2.5	No major errors or omissions regarding score 2.0 content, and partial success at score 3.0 content
Score 2.0	There are no major errors or omissions regarding the simpler details and processes as the student: • *Recognizes or recalls specific terminology, such as* chronological • *Performs basic processes, such as describing relevant past and present events*
Score 1.5	Partial success at score 2.0 content, and major errors or omissions regarding score 3.0 content
Score 1.0	With help, the student will achieve partial success at score 2.0 content and score 3.0 content.
Score 0.5	With help, partial success at score 2.0 content but not at score 3.0 content
Score 0.0	Even with help, the student has no success.

Source: © 2021 by South Sioux City Community Schools. Used with permission.

Figure 1.4: Sample proficiency scale for high school social studies.

You may notice that these scales include half-point scores. These help you and your students in many ways. As a teacher, you can measure student knowledge more precisely. Students who receive a half-point score have demonstrated knowledge that is between two levels. There are many times a student may know and do all of the 2.0 knowledge and skills and some of the score 3.0 content but still struggle with a few of the 3.0 learning targets. Score 2.5 reflects that a student has demonstrated proficiency with simpler content and demonstrated some understanding of the target content. The equivalent would be true at the 3.5 level; a student has mastered the proficiency learning targets and is working on the more advanced content. Using half points on the proficiency scale helps students see their progress and inspires them to keep working.

The content listed at levels 2.0 and 3.0 of the proficiency scale, being directly related to the priority standard, represents content that is essential—in other words, content that will be taught and assessed. The essential nature of the priority standard and the proficiency scale in terms of student development along the learning progression represented in the scale means that content at levels 2.0 and 3.0 is not optional. The 4.0 content is optional; not every student will be expected to master the 4.0 content and knowledge.

It is important to note that the score 4.0 learning target lists a sample task or two that the student could perform to show advanced understanding and skill. The learning target does not include specific content. This is a fundamental difference from the learning targets at scores 2.0 and 3.0. Teachers do not provide instruction at the 4.0 level; there is no specific 4.0 material. In some scales, rather than specifying a task, score 4.0 may simply state that students will demonstrate in-depth inferences and applications. However, we recommend that score 4.0 list at least one sample task. Doing so serves three purposes. First, listing sample tasks provides some tangible ideas for how students may go beyond the proficient expectation. Second, it helps you as an individual teacher plan for differentiating learning and prevents having to generate those ideas on the fly. Third, it increases consistency among you and your teammates.

Whether the proficiency scale you develop includes a sample task at level 4.0 or a more general description of beyond-proficient ability, you should plan to offer activities that allow students to show 4.0 performance. Whatever activity or activities you provide, they must require new thinking on the part of the student, and the cognitive demand must be equal to the examples given in the proficiency scale, though the particular activity may vary.

In a standards-based learning environment, proficiency scales form the basis of instruction, assessment, feedback, and grading. Teachers deliver instruction based on the expectations and progressions that proficiency scales define. Assessments align to scales, and students receive feedback on their performance that clearly describes where they are on the scale. Ideally, teachers report grades on the four-point scale, rather than using letter grades or percentages. The proficiency scale also forms the foundation for a consistent system centered on student learning. It is the centerpiece of communication and understanding in the classroom, as well as the common language for discussing learning between teacher and student, as demonstrated in figure 1.5 (page 20). This graphic visually depicts how the proficiency scale anchors the learning environment. It appears in the center of the graphic because it serves as the foundation for all the surrounding related concepts: planning, instruction, assessment, and feedback. The graphic also signifies that proficiency scales are used not only by the teacher, but also by students. Students use proficiency scales to guide their understanding of grade-level or course expectations.

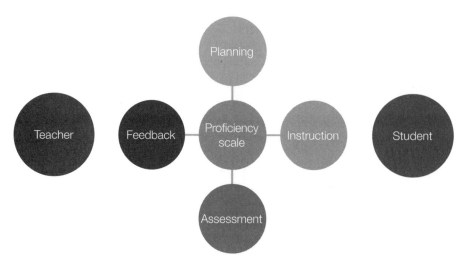

Source: Heflebower et al., 2019, p. 10.

Figure 1.5: The role of the proficiency scale in classroom communication and understanding.

Developing Proficiency Scales

There are various ways to construct a proficiency scale. We detail several methods in the upcoming sections: (1) customizing existing scales, (2) creating new scales using the standards as target content, and (3) creating new scales using a five-step process. First, however, there are three decisions we suggest you make prior to scale development (Heflebower, Hoegh, & Warrick, 2021).

1. **Will these scales include score 0.0?** While 0.0 on a proficiency scale indicates that a student cannot demonstrate understanding even with help from the teacher, people sometimes confuse it with a traditional zero (indicating that a student has done no work or failed to turn in the assignment). To prevent this confusion, some educators decide to omit the 0.0 level from their scales.

2. **Will these scales include half-point scores?** As mentioned previously, half-point scores offer more precision in grading and allow students to see more frequent incremental progress. Some teachers may find it easier to begin without half-point scores, but we suggest you consider them.

3. **How will we approach score 4.0 content on these scales?** Some experts suggest that the target content (score 3.0) should be the highest level of the scale (O'Connor, 2018; Schimmer, 2016). The score 4.0 level, however, offers opportunities for students to go beyond proficiency. Some educators simply list a boilerplate statement such as, "In addition to score 3.0, in-depth inferences and applications that go beyond what was taught," but it can be helpful to list one or two samples of level 4.0 performance to guide students and teachers, as we previously recommended.

With these decisions in mind, you can use one of the following approaches to develop proficiency scales for a course or content area. A manageable set of twelve to fifteen proficiency scales for each grade level and subject area defines a curriculum that is both guaranteed and viable—guaranteed in that it is consistent across classrooms and viable in that there is enough instructional time to address all the content (Heflebower et al., 2021). Sometimes the number of scales an individual teacher or team develops for a grade level or course is fewer, however, and sometimes the number is greater. For instance, U.S. history teachers often find it difficult to narrow their content, and may initially have more proficiency scales due to the nature of their course. For more detail on creating scales, consult *A Handbook for Developing and Using Proficiency Scales in the Classroom* (Hoegh, 2020).

Customize Existing Scales

One option for developing proficiency scales is to customize existing proficiency scales. It is important that any teacher or team of teachers considers scales from an outside source (like other districts or commercial products) as starter scales, meaning that they need to be customized for the team's particular school or district. If you are just beginning the scale-development process, you might work with or refer to another school or district that has already developed scales, perhaps even using some of their scales as a starting point for your own work. Referencing others' work reduces your workload as you can just add or delete information, as opposed to coming up with it entirely yourself. You simply review an existing scale and determine what is appropriate for your classroom. Alternatively, as mentioned in the previous section, there are commercially available scales, such as those associated with the Marzano Resources Critical Concepts (Marzano Resources, n.d.a). These are topic-based proficiency scales that require customization of the score 2.0 content. The analysts intentionally crafted these scales with a plethora of options listed at the 2.0 level, for the express purpose of teachers' customizing them.

When reviewing and revising scales for customization, look for alignment between your 2.0 and 3.0 learning targets. Ensure that the vocabulary and basic facts and skills listed are sufficient to support students' reaching proficiency at the score 3.0 level. You may also find that you want different wording within the scale. By all means, personalize the scales to be useful. For instance, you may prefer to combine statements that seem redundant or expand on others as needed. Some teachers refrain from using the verb *understand* as they believe it to be too vague; they often use *know and describe* in its place. You might also adjust terms to reflect local usage—different states and provinces reference standards a bit differently. For instance, some places use the phrase *year 1* instead of *grade 1* and so on.

To customize scales, review each proficiency scale to determine the following.

1. Identify content that should be directly taught and assessed. Bold or underline these.

2. Identify content that is often taught and assessed with another learning target. Combine these and strike through the original.

3. Identify content that is so general as to be implicit in other learning targets. Delete these.

The result should be three to five score 2.0 learning targets per score 3.0 learning target and a list of critical vocabulary. Figures 1.6 and 1.7 (pages 22 and 23) depict the customization process.

Generating Text Organization and Structure (Kindergarten ELA)

4.0	The student will: • Create a title for a text that relates to the text's main topic (for example, after writing a draft about several different kinds of fish that live in the ocean, decide that a good title would be *Fish in the Ocean*). • Use a graphic organizer to plan out which information to include in a text.
3.5	In addition to score 3.0 performance, partial success at score 4.0 content
3.0	The student will: **GTOS1—State the topic of a text** (for example, write or explain that the topic of a text is *animals that live in the ocean*). **GTOS2—Use drawing, dictating, and writing to supply information about a topic** (for example, provide information about fish that live in the ocean by listing some kinds of fish that live in the ocean, explaining what each kind of fish eats, and including an illustration that shows what each kind of fish looks like).
2.5	No major errors or omission regarding score 2.0 content, and partial success at score 3.0 content
2.0	GTOS1—The student will recognize or recall specific vocabulary (for example, **about**, **illustration**, **information**, **match**, *opinion*, *story*, **topic**, *word*, *write*) and perform basic processes such as: • Explain that a topic is what a text is about. State that the words and illustrations in a text should be about the same topic. • ~~State that the words and illustrations in a text should be about the same topic.~~ • ~~List~~ STATE possible topics for a text. • ~~Identify whether a text should tell a story about a topic.~~ **Students explain that a text shares information about a topic,** ~~or give an opinion on a topic.~~ **Not whether or not they like the topic.** • ~~Fill in a sentence stem~~ **State a word or short phrase that identifies the topic of a text** (for example, fill in the phrase *Today I learned about _____* with the topic of a text). (Standard says *state*, not *identify*) GTOS2—The student will recognize or recall specific vocabulary (for example, *detail*, *fact*, *information*, **people**, **place**, *relate*, **sketch**, *topic*) and perform basic processes such as: • ~~List~~ **Draw, dictate, or write known facts or information about a topic.** • **Identify people, animals, or objects that relate to a topic.** • **Identify places that relate to a topic.** • **Identify whether a detail or piece of information relates to a specific topic.** • ~~Use a graphic organizer to plan out which information to include in a text.~~ • ~~Sketch details that relate to a topic.~~ (Redundant)
1.5	Partial success at score 2.0 content, and major errors or omissions regarding score 3.0 content
1.0	With help, partial success at score 2.0 content and score 3.0 content
0.5	With help, partial success at score 2.0 content but not at score 3.0 content
0.0	Even with help, no success

Side annotations:

I determined vocabulary essential for each element in 3.0. I bolded them.

I combined (then struck through) those learning targets that were redundant. I matched the verb to what the standard was referencing (*state*) as opposed to substituting another.

I bolded the remaining learning targets that will be taught and assessed for this measurement topic.

Source: Adapted from Marzano Resources, n.d.a.

Figure 1.6: Customizing a kindergarten proficiency scale.

Measures of Central Tendency (Grade 6 Mathematics)

4.0	The student will: • Predict the ways in which a data set's measures of central tendency might change with the addition or removal of certain data points (for example, when given the set of numbers {1, 1, 5, 7, 9, 13}, predict what would happen to the set's measures of central tendency if the lowest and highest values were to be removed).
3.5	In addition to score 3.0 performance, partial success at score 4.0 content
3.0	The student will: **MCT1—Calculate the mean of a data set** (for example, when given the set of numbers {7, 7, 2.3, $\frac{7}{2}$, 2($\frac{3}{4}$), $\frac{1}{4}$, 5, 0}, calculate the arithmetic mean of the set). **MCT2—Calculate the median of a data set** (for example, when given the set of numbers {7, 7, 2.3, $\frac{7}{2}$, 2($\frac{3}{4}$), $\frac{1}{4}$, 5, 0}, calculate the median of the set). **MCT3—Calculate the mode of a data set** (for example, when given the set of numbers {7, 7, 2.3, $\frac{7}{2}$, 2($\frac{3}{4}$), $\frac{1}{4}$, 5, 0}, calculate the modes of the set).
2.5	No major errors or omissions regarding score 2.0 content, and partial success at score 3.0 content
2.0	MCT1—The student will recognize or recall specific vocabulary (for example, *arithmetic mean*, ***average***, *cluster*, *data point*, ***data set***, *extreme*, ***mean***, ***measure of central tendency***, *ordered list*, *outlier*) and perform basic processes such as: • **Explain that a measure of central tendency is a means of representing or summarizing an entire data set with a single number.** (Keep as is) • Explain that the mean of a data set can be calculated by adding together every data point in the set and then dividing the sum by the number of data points in the set. (Combined with bullet below) • **Explain that the arithmetic mean is what people are typically referring to when they speak of an "average," and it can be calculated by adding points in the data set and dividing by the number of data points.** • **Explain that the mean of a set can be affected by data points that are significantly different from the rest of the data points in the set—outliers.** (Added the term) MCT2—The student will recognize or recall specific vocabulary (for example, *cluster*, *data point*, *data set*, *extreme*, *mean*, *measure of central tendency*, ***median***, ***middle number***, ***ordered list***, *outlier*) and perform basic processes such as: • Explain that a measure of central tendency is a means of representing or summarizing an entire data set with a single number. (Already addressed above) • Order the data points of a data set from least to greatest. (Redundant) • **Explain that the median of a data set is the middle data point in the set when the data points are placed in order from least to greatest.** (Keep as is) • **Explain that the median of a data set with an even number of data points can be determined by calculating the mean of the middle two data points in the set (the value halfway between those data points).** (Keep as is) • **Explain that the median of a set is not affected as much as the mean by data points that are significantly different from the rest of the data points in the set.** (Keep as is) MCT3—The student will recognize or recall specific vocabulary (for example, *cluster*, *data point*, *data set*, *extreme*, *measure of central tendency*, ***mode***, ***ordered list***, *outlier*) and perform basic processes such as: • Explain that a measure of central tendency is a means of representing or summarizing an entire data set with a single number. (Redundant) • **Explain that the mode of a data set is the most common data point in the set.** • **Explain that a data set may have no mode, one mode, or more than one mode.**

Sidebar notes:

I determined vocabulary essential for each element in 3.0. I bolded them.

I combined (then struck through) those learning targets that were redundant.

I bolded the remaining learning targets that will be taught and assessed for this measurement topic.

Source: Adapted from Marzano Resources, n.d.a.

Figure 1.7: Customizing a sixth-grade proficiency scale.

In summary, the customization process lessens the burden of deriving the contents of the scale from the standards yet ensures that the teachers who will be using the scales personalize them. Using the Critical Concepts or other existing scales as a starting point can expedite the scale-development process. It is also possible and probable that you can insert supporting standards you identified earlier as learning targets for either the 2.0 or 3.0 levels on a proficiency scale for a priority standard. For instance, you may have two or three related supporting standards that you can use as learning targets within a proficiency scale. If you elect to use preexisting proficiency scales as the basis of your work, simply ensure that you take time to read, review, and revise them.

Create New Scales Using the Standards as Target Content

While customizing existing proficiency scales is one effective and efficient method for scale development, another option is to design proficiency scales on your own. One common method we suggest is to record the priority standard (in its entirety) at the score 3.0 level on the proficiency scale. From there, the teacher or teacher team determines essential vocabulary and other simple content (knowledge and skills considered foundational to the 3.0 learning targets) and records it at score 2.0. Lastly, the teacher would generate a sample application task for score 4.0. This process is a bit more basic than the one in the next section but is a great starting point.

This approach often works well at the elementary level, as elementary standards tend to be a bit less complicated and have fewer specific learning targets embedded within them. However, at the secondary level, standards are often more expansive and cumbersome. In other words, secondary standards may be multidimensional—there may be numerous learning targets that do not covary within a single priority standard. If you employ the method of using standards as target content, be mindful of that consideration.

Create New Scales Using a Five-Step Process

Another scale-development method uses a five-step process to determine each score level on the proficiency scale. The steps are as follows (Hoegh, 2020).

1. Determine the topic of the proficiency scale.

2. Determine the language of score 3.0 (the target content).

3. Determine vocabulary related to the target content and record it at score 2.0 (the simpler content).

4. Determine basic knowledge and skills and record them at score 2.0.

5. Identify an example or two of how a student might demonstrate score 4.0 performance (the more complex content).

Consider this grade 2 reading standard: "The student will recount stories, including fables and folktales from diverse cultures, and determine their central message, lesson, or moral" (RL.2.2, NGA & CCSSO, 2010a). The following thought process might be used in association with each step in the five-step process.

1. **Determine the topic of the proficiency scale.** Teachers creating a proficiency scale for this standard might think, "This standard is all

about determining the central idea of a text. We will call it 'Determining Central Idea.'"

2. **Determine the language of score 3.0.** Again, teachers following this process might think, "The language of the standard is fine, except it might be helpful to make it more concise and use our usual bulleted format. Reformatting it in this way would make clear the most important skill—determining the central message, lesson, or moral."

The student will:

- Determine the central message or moral of stories, fables, and folktales.

3. **Determine vocabulary related to the target content and record it in score 2.0.** Again, teachers considering the important vocabulary terms might think, "The standard provides some important terminology, but we should add a couple of terms that are important as we teach this skill. They will need to recognize or recall specific terminology such as *central idea, fable, folktale, message, lesson, moral, hero, heroine.*"

4. **Determine basic knowledge and skills and record them in score 2.0.** In considering what must be in place for the students to work on the standard at score 3.0, teachers might think, "Students will definitely need to be able to retell the text in question, and they will also need a process for identifying central message, an important stepping-stone to determining central message."

- Accurately retell stories from diverse cultures, including fables and folktales.

- Understand a process for determining central message from a text.

5. **Identify an example or two of how a student might demonstrate a score 4.0 performance.** Again, the thought process might go as follows: "There are numerous ways a student could demonstrate going beyond proficiency. What if we gave them multiple texts and asked them not only to determine the central messages of the texts but also to account for similarities and differences in the messages?"

The proficiency scale in figure 1.8 (page 26) is a product of the five-step process.

Summary

In this chapter, we have discussed the underlying curriculum work that enables teachers to begin planning and instructing based on standards. While standards prioritization and proficiency scale development may occur at the school or district level, it is important for individual teachers to understand these processes. With a viable set of standards and high-quality proficiency scales in hand, you can now proceed to the next step of the planning process: determining the sequence and timing of instruction throughout the learning period. As such, developing curriculum maps based on standards and scales is the subject of our next chapter.

Determining Central Idea	
Priority Standard: The student will recount stories, including fables and folktales from diverse cultures, and determine their central message, lesson, or moral. (RL.2.2)	
Score 4.0	The student will: • Explain patterns in the central messages of several texts from diverse cultures
Score 3.0	The student will: • Determine the central message or moral of stories, fables, and folktales
Score 2.0	The student will: • Recognize or recall specific terminology such as *central idea*, *fable*, *folktale*, *message*, *lesson*, *moral*, *hero*, *heroine* • Accurately retell stories from diverse cultures, including fables and folktales • Understand a process for determining central message from a text
Score 1.0	With help, partial success at score 2.0 content and score 3.0 content

Source: Adapted from Marzano et al., 2013.

Source for standard: NGA & CCSSO, 2010a.

Figure 1.8: Proficiency scale created using the five-step process.

2

Year-Long Planning With Curriculum Maps

Once they have prioritized standards and developed proficiency scales, teachers or teams of teachers are positioned to engage in effective instructional planning. There are three phases of standards-based instructional planning, and all are paramount for ensuring high-quality classroom instruction.

1. Curriculum mapping (year- or course-long planning)

2. Instructional cycle planning (unit planning)

3. Daily lesson planning

This chapter will focus on curriculum mapping, which involves planning for the scope of the year or course, while chapter 3 (page 37) explores unit planning and chapter 4 (page 65) addresses daily lesson planning.

With proficiency scales developed, it is necessary to determine when each of the proficiency scales will receive instructional focus. The process of curriculum mapping involves identifying when and for approximately how long to teach each scale. As we begin the discussion of year- or course-long planning, recall that a guaranteed and viable curriculum usually consists of about twelve to fifteen proficiency scales per course or content area and grade level. Whatever the number of scales, teachers must plan the most logical order for teaching the content on the proficiency scales to students.

The curriculum mapping process has numerous benefits for teachers and students. The greatest benefit to teachers is clarity about when and for how long to teach the contents of each proficiency scale. For example, a fourth-grade teacher might decide through the curriculum mapping process that he will teach the proficiency scale for place value in mathematics for the first three weeks of the academic year. Teachers also gain insight about what parts of their curriculum resources are relevant to teaching the content on their proficiency scales. To continue the previous example, the curriculum mapping process might help this fourth-grade teacher discover which sections or chapters in the mathematics textbook support the teaching of the learning targets on the place-value proficiency scale. Teachers often find that their textbooks contain unneeded pages, sections, or even chapters as they engage in the curriculum mapping process. With this knowledge, they can devote their time effectively to the material that best aligns with the standards.

Students also benefit from the clarity that results from curriculum mapping. They understand what they need to know and be able to do throughout the entirety of an academic year or course because the curriculum map makes public the topic of each instructional unit. For example, when a teacher knows that the proficiency scale on solving quadratic equations will be the instructional focus for approximately twelve class periods, he or she can communicate a learning target from the proficiency scale to students at the beginning of each class period to ensure they know the current focus for learning. Teachers' clear communication about what students must know and be able to do positively impacts student achievement, relating to as much as a 27-percentile-point gain in student achievement (Corwin & SmartBrief, 2017; Hattie, 2009).

Curriculum maps will likely differ in nuanced ways between content areas, simply because of the differences in the nature of the material. For example, English language arts is a content area that lends itself nicely to standards spiraling back around numerous times over the course of an academic year. To illustrate, perhaps in grade 2 ELA the priority standard for main idea and supporting details is taught multiple times throughout an academic year. In fact, it may be instructionally addressed in any lesson involving informational texts, therefore providing students multiple opportunities to acquire the knowledge and skills encompassed within the standard. As a result of this spiraling, some standards will appear numerous times within the curriculum map. Other content areas, such as mathematics, are more linear in nature, so each standard might appear only once in the curriculum map. When this is the case, teachers must create opportunities to revisit those standards to ensure that all students have multiple opportunities to attain mastery and to review topics for better retention. For example, consider again a fourth-grade curriculum map for mathematics. The topic of place value is the emphasis for the first unit of instruction. The second unit is focused on addition and subtraction. The teacher should plan to reinforce the place-value standards in a variety of ways to ensure that students maintain the knowledge and skills encompassed in the standards taught in that unit. Some teachers use bell ringers or exit slips for this reinforcement. Others intentionally plan intermittent review times in their daily instruction. Regardless of the strategy used, when the content is more linear than spiraling, planning opportunities to reinforce previously taught priority standards must be part of the instructional process.

In this chapter, we describe three methods of curriculum mapping.

1. Curriculum mapping based on a curriculum resource
2. Curriculum mapping based on existing instructional units
3. Curriculum mapping based on proficiency scales

The following sections detail each method in turn. An individual teacher can use one of these methods to map his or her curriculum. However, when possible, we encourage teachers to work collaboratively. A higher degree of instructional consistency results when teams of teachers work together on curriculum mapping and instructional cycle planning (see chapter 3, page 37). The *guaranteed* aspect of a guaranteed and viable curriculum means eliminating variability in student learning between classrooms so, for example, students in one tenth-grade classroom learn the same content as students in another tenth-grade classroom, regardless of the teacher to whom they have been assigned. This consistency in *what* will be taught still allows a high degree of teacher autonomy because there are no requirements for *how* the content is taught. In fact, none of the three methods described address how content is to be taught, making the curriculum mapping process one that most educators view as very beneficial.

Curriculum Mapping Based on a Curriculum Resource

It is very common for teachers to use a textbook or other preexisting curriculum resource to support the instructional process. Historically, some teachers relied heavily on textbooks, sometimes even following the scope and sequence of a textbook cover to cover. With proficiency scales in place, a textbook can truly become a resource, rather than the primary document, for planning instruction across the entirety of an academic year or course. While an individual teacher can successfully complete this process, it works best when conducted by a small team of teachers for a particular grade level or course. Curriculum mapping based on a curriculum resource includes the following steps.

1. **Examine the curriculum resource (such as a textbook) to identify the proficiency scales and specific learning targets that each chapter addresses.** This step requires a thorough examination of each chapter within the textbook in tandem with each of the proficiency scales for the grade level or course to determine where the two align.

2. **Create a document that charts the findings from step 1.** This might look like a table with a row for each standard and a column for each textbook chapter. Teachers can check off the chapters where each standard appears or record the sections within the chapter for added specificity. Figure 2.1 displays an example where the teachers have listed the section numbers that correspond to each standard.

3. **Review the results to determine whether or not all priority standards are represented in at least one chapter of the textbook or curriculum resource.** If not, indicate which standards are missing and plan to determine how you will support instruction for these standards.

Priority Standard	Chapter 1	Chapter 2	Chapter 3	Chapter 4	Chapter 5	Chapter 6
RL.5.1: Quote accurately from a literary text			3, 4, 9, 11, 12	1, 4, 5, 6, 9, 12, 14		2
RL.5.2: Determine theme		5, 6, 7	1, 2, 3, 5, 6, 7, 8, 9, 10, 12	11, 12		2, 3, 5
RL.5.5: Story structure				1, 3, 4		2

Figure 2.1: Curriculum map for grade 5 ELA based on a textbook.

continued →

Priority Standard	Chapter 1	Chapter 2	Chapter 3	Chapter 4	Chapter 5	Chapter 6
RI.5.1: Quote accurately from an informational text	2, 3, 6, 7, 11, 13, 14	1, 2, 3, 8, 9, 12			1, 2, 3, 5, 10	1, 3, 5, 6, 7, 9
RI.5.2: Main idea		1, 2, 3, 4, 8, 9, 10, 11, 12			7, 8	1, 3, 5, 6, 7, 9
RI.5.3: Relationships within a text	4, 5	1, 2			1, 4, 6, 11, 12	1, 3, 5, 6, 7, 9
RI.5.5: Overall structure						
W.5.1: Opinion writing				2, 3, 4, 5		
W.5.2: Informative writing		3, 6, 7, 10, 12		2, 3, 4, 5, 10	3, 4, 5, 8, 10, 12, 13, 17	7, 8, 5, 10

Source for standards: NGA & CCSSO, 2010a.

Once you've mapped the curriculum based on your textbook or other curriculum resource, you can follow the scope and sequence prescribed by the author or vendor. As you teach each chapter in the textbook, emphasize the content addressed on your proficiency scales. The learning targets on each proficiency scale that are covered in the chapter receive specific focus in an effort to ensure that all students master the priority standards. In the end, both the curriculum resource and the proficiency scales are used to promote high levels of student learning.

There are multiple benefits to curriculum mapping based on a curriculum resource. First of all, the workload for teachers is minimized in terms of finding support materials for teaching the content on proficiency scales. Most curriculum resources provide a plethora of support materials to choose from, including reproducible documents, assessments, slide sets, and so on. Second, most textbooks are carefully designed to present content to students in a logical order. When following the textbook, teachers can be confident that they address the necessary foundational skills before teaching something that requires higher-level skills. For teachers newer to the profession or unsure of their content expertise, reliance on a curriculum resource provides necessary support. Lastly, this method honors a school's or district's investment in the curriculum resource. The adoption of any curriculum resource is a time-consuming and costly endeavor. By using the curriculum resource as the basis for curriculum mapping and instruction throughout the academic year or course, the time and financial resources invested are greatly worthwhile.

Curriculum Mapping Based on Existing Instructional Units

The concept of developing and teaching instructional units is not new to the classroom. Many teachers who are accustomed to planning and teaching based on content can adjust to a standards-based approach with this method. Some teachers enjoy the instructional unit design process and would rather plan instruction without reliance on any particular curriculum resource. Instead, they create units that span a period of time and address a standard or a small cluster of related standards. For example, a team of sixth-grade science teachers works collaboratively to design a collection of instructional units to be taught over the course of an academic year. Then, they review the priority standards for sixth-grade science and align them with the units to ensure students will have opportunities to learn all the important content.

Curriculum mapping based on existing instructional units includes the following steps.

1. **List the units of instruction that are typically taught during the academic year in the order in which they are taught.** It is helpful to list the title of each existing instructional unit in the left-hand column of a table or template.

2. **Determine the priority and supporting standards that are addressed in each existing unit of instruction.** Record these standards in the template. It is helpful to indicate the priority standards in some way, such as using bold-face font.

3. **Review the results to determine whether all priority standards are represented in at least one unit of instruction.** If not, identify which standards are missing and plan to address instruction for these standards.

Figure 2.2 (page 32) displays a portion of a grade 6 curriculum map for science. The map presents the titles of existing units of instruction, as well as the standards that are addressed within each unit. The map also provides information about pacing—the amount of time to be spent teaching each unit. Because the map is based on existing units that the teacher has previously taught, the amount of time to be spent teaching the unit is based on this previous experience. Finally, the map lists supporting materials for providing high-quality opportunities to learn the content. Since no specific textbook or other curriculum resource serves as the basis for each unit, teachers typically supplement their teaching with resources they have either developed or acquired over time. Sometimes curriculum maps are digital documents that include hyperlinks to other online or virtually stored documents related to the unit, including the supporting materials.

One of the most favorable aspects of basing a curriculum map on existing units of instruction is the level of teacher autonomy. Teachers are not required to follow the scope and sequence of any particular resource; instead, they determine the most logical order for teaching the content on the proficiency scales for the grade level or course. You may find you like this method because it honors your decision-making ability and content expertise.

Additionally, this method is based on previously completed instructional unit design, which recognizes past efforts and reduces new work to be done. This does not mean that existing units of instruction don't change as a result of newly developed proficiency scales. Typically, the inclusion of proficiency scales and standards enhances existing instructional units, as scales showcase the most critical content, which the teacher then ensures receives adequate instructional focus.

Title of Unit	Standards in Unit	Pacing	Supporting Materials
Human Energy	**MS-PS3-1. Construct and interpret graphical displays of data to describe the relationships of kinetic energy to the mass of an object, and to the speed of an object.** **MS-PS3-2. Develop a model to describe that when the arrangement of objects interacting at a distance changes, different amounts of potential energy are stored in the system.** MS-PS3-5. Construct, use, and present arguments to support the claim that when the kinetic energy of an object changes, energy is transferred to or from the object.	15 to 17 days	• Potential Predictions Lab • Scientist Report Form • Scientist Outline
Force and Motion	**MS-PS2-1. Apply Newton's third law to design a solution to a problem involving the motion of two colliding objects.** MS-PS2-2. Plan an investigation to provide evidence that the change in an object's motion depends on the sum of the forces on the object and the mass of the object. **MS-PS3-1. Construct and interpret graphical displays of data to describe the relationships of kinetic energy to the mass of an object, and to the speed of an object.**	23 to 25 days	• Speed and Motion Lab • Heel-Toe Activity • Gravity and Space Simulation (PhET Interactive Simulation) • Gravity and Orbits Simulation (PhET Interactive Simulation) • Ball Drop Activity

Source: © 2021 by Uinta County School District #1. Used with permission.
Source for standards: NGSS Lead States, 2013.

Figure 2.2: Curriculum map for grade 6 science based on instructional units.

Curriculum Mapping Based on Proficiency Scales

The third method for curriculum mapping involves considering all the proficiency scales for a particular grade level or course and determining the order and pacing. Rather than matching standards and scales to existing resources or units, this method allows teachers to build a curriculum map from the scales themselves. While individual teachers can use this method, it works best when approached by a team of three to five content experts. Thus, we recommend this method when no single specific curriculum resource is required for use across a school district or system of schools, but leaders want to provide instructional guidance to individual teachers in their school, district, or system of schools.

Use the following steps to conduct curriculum mapping based on proficiency scales.

1. **Divide the academic year or duration of the course into increments of time.** Most academic years are thirty-six weeks long. Some teams simply divide the year into equal increments of time. For example, a second-grade team might decide to have six six-week increments for teaching the content

on their proficiency scales in English language arts. Other teams may decide to vary their increments of time. Perhaps a ninth-grade mathematics team divides the academic year into nine segments ranging from one week to six weeks. Segmenting the academic year or course is simply a function of what the team determines is best for their particular situation. In the end, each increment of time will be the duration of a unit or instructional cycle.

2. **Determine the primary instructional focus for each unit or instructional cycle.** For each increment of time established in step 1, identify the main topic of the instructional unit. For example, a team of second-grade teachers might determine that the academic year will begin with an instructional focus on informational and literary texts in ELA, including the concepts of text features and story structures. Following this instructional cycle, the focus changes to author's purpose and point of view. This step of curriculum mapping will take significant time. However, it is well worth the time, as it sets the team up for success in step 3.

3. **Identify the proficiency scales to be taught within each instructional cycle.** Once you have identified the instructional focus of each unit, it is time to assign scales to each increment of time. The scales included within each unit are those that relate most closely to the primary focus determined in step 2. It is best practice (but not a requirement) to also include the relevant supporting standards since teachers are required to address both in the classroom. It is also helpful to offer the topic of each proficiency scale in the curriculum map, as well as an abbreviated version of the supporting standards so that teachers can easily identify the essence of the scales and standards included within any unit as they examine the document.

The curriculum map in figure 2.3 (page 34) is a portion of a grade 2 ELA example based on proficiency scales. The team of teachers elected to divide the academic year into equal increments of time, resulting in six six-week units of instruction. The focus of each unit is represented in the map by the rows labeled *Genre* and *Big Idea*. The decisions for the focus of each unit are made by the teacher or teacher teams creating the map and are based on their content expertise and experience. Obviously, they want to teach the knowledge and skills on the proficiency scales in the most logical order possible and to allocate adequate time for each scale. Finally, the team decided to include priority and supporting standards for each of the ELA domains (Reading Literary and Informational, Reading Foundational, Writing, and Language) for each unit. In this example, each priority standard has a correlating proficiency scale. The end result is a framework for planning instruction across the course of an academic year or the duration of a course.

It is important to note that steps 2 (determine the primary instructional focus for each unit or instructional cycle) and 3 (identify the proficiency scales to be taught within each instructional cycle) may be reversed in using this method for curriculum mapping. In the case that a team chooses this option, they simply consider all of the available proficiency scales and group scales that make logical sense to teach within the same increment of

Grade 2 Curriculum Map					
Unit and Timeline	**Unit 1** **First Six Weeks**		**Unit 2** **Second Six Weeks**		**Unit 3** **Third Six Weeks**
Genre	Literary and Informational		Literary and Informational		Literacy
Big Idea	Text Features and Story Structures		Author's Purpose and Point of View		Key Ideas and Details
Reading Literary and Informational Standards	Priority: 2.RI.CAS.5— Text features 2.RL.CAS.5— Story structure	Supporting: N/A	Priority: 2.RI.CAS.6— Purpose of text	Supporting: 2.RL.CAS.6— Point of view	Priority: 2.RL.KID.1— Ask and answer questions 2.RL.KID.3— Major events	Supporting: 2.RL.KID.2— Recount stories
Reading Foundational Standards	Priority: 2.RF.PWR.3— Decoding 2.RF.FLU.4— Fluency	Supporting: 2.SL.CAC.1— Collaborative conversations	Priority: 2.RF.PWR.3— Decoding 2.RF.FLU.4— Fluency	Supporting: 2.SL.CAC.1— Collaborative conversations	Priority: 2.RF.PWR.3— Decoding 2.RF.FLU.4— Fluency	Supporting: 2.L.VAU.6— Use words and phrases 2.L.KOL.3— Conventions of language
Writing Standards	Priority: 2.W.TTP.3— Narrative 2.W.PDW.5— Writing process	Supporting: 2.L.KOL.3— Conventions of language	Priority: 2.W.RBK.8— Recall information from experiences 2.W.RBK.7— Participate in shared research	Supporting: 2.L.VAU.6— Use words and phrases 2.W.PDW.6— Digital publishing	Priority: 2.W.PDW.5— Writing process	Supporting: 2.W.TTP.1— Opinion
Language Standards	Priority: 2.L.CSE.1— Grammar and usage when writing and speaking	Supporting: 2.L.KOL.3— Conventions of language	Priority: 2.L.CSE.1— Grammar and usage when writing and speaking	Supporting: 2.L.KOL.3— Conventions of language 2.L.VAU.6— Use words and phrases	Priority: 2.L.CSE.2— Capitalization, punctuation, and spelling when writing	Supporting: 2.L.VAU.4— Meaning of unknown words

Source: © 2021 by Archdiocese of Chicago. Used with permission.
Source for standards: Archdiocese of Chicago, n.d.a.

Figure 2.3: Sample curriculum map.

time. For example, a grade 2 team might group the scales for the topics of text features, central idea, and connections together for a four-week instructional cycle. The decision to include these three scales in the same time period is based on the fact that all three scales are about informational text. Following this decision, they title the unit "A Study of Informational Text." The team then plans other instructional units to be taught across the second-grade year.

A benefit of curriculum mapping based on proficiency scales is that it provides guidance for *what* is to be taught during increments of time. This leads to consistency across classrooms within a school and even schools across a district or system of schools in that all teachers for a particular grade or course are addressing the same standards at the same time. Teachers typically appreciate such guidance, especially because they retain freedom in *how* they teach the content.

Summary

This chapter has presented information about the importance of curriculum mapping and three possible methods for completing this critical work. Regardless of the method you choose, the curriculum mapping process results in guidance for instruction throughout an academic year or course. Further, it does so in a way that each priority standard receives adequate instructional focus, thereby increasing the likelihood that students will master the content. Teachers should note that regardless of which curriculum-mapping method their school or team adopts, teachers still retain the autonomy of choosing *how* they will teach the required instructional cycles. The next step in the planning process is the development of the instructional cycle or unit. We address that in the next chapter.

3

Unit Planning With the Instructional Cycle

At the beginning of chapter 2 (page 27), we stated that there are three phases of instructional planning: year-long planning, instructional cycle planning, and daily lesson planning. Now that we have addressed year- or course-long planning in chapter 2, it is time to move to the next phase. This second phase of planning is an extension of the year- or course-long planning process that occurs in phase one. It involves using the curriculum map to plan instructional cycles, which will ultimately lead to daily lessons, which we will address in chapter 4 (page 65).

An instructional cycle is simply an increment of time within the academic year or course spent teaching important related academic content to students. Some teachers use the term instructional *unit* rather than *cycle* for these increments of time. We chose the word *cycle* to emphasize the idea that each increment of time within the academic year or course includes a series of steps that are repeated in the same order. In other words, a teacher or team of teachers engages in the same set of activities during each increment of time. Each instructional cycle includes one or more priority standards and typically a few supporting standards. The number of standards included impacts the amount of time spent in the cycle, but most are a week to six weeks in length.

The following eight steps make up the instructional cycle.

1. Identifying the focus of the instructional cycle

2. Reviewing the relevant standards and proficiency scales included in the cycle

3. Planning to collect evidence of student learning (preassessments, formative checks for understanding, and summative assessments)

4. Writing a SMART goal

5. Planning and teaching the daily lessons within the cycle

6. Administering and scoring the end-of-cycle assessment

7. Implementing the assessment data protocol to analyze the assessment results

8. Providing support for all learners based on the end-of-cycle assessment data

We can represent these eight steps as a recursive cycle, as shown in figure 3.1, because they are revisited with each instructional cycle. The cycle occurs multiple times throughout the course or academic year. Initial planning for each cycle (that is, the first four steps) may occur at different times, depending on the preferences of the teacher or team of teachers and availability of time. One option is for the first four steps to occur prior to the end of the previous instructional cycle so that the teacher is prepared to make a seamless transition from one cycle to the next. Another option is to take significant time prior to the start of the academic year to plan all instructional cycles. The important thing to remember about the first four steps is that they occur prior to teaching the content in the instructional cycle.

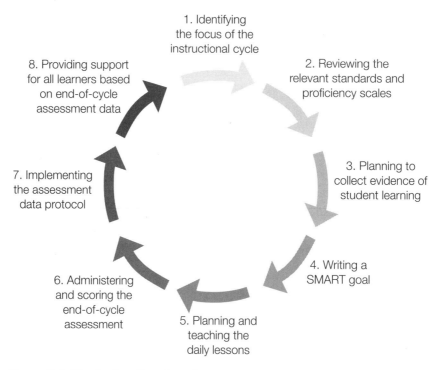

Figure 3.1: The instructional cycle.

The primary purpose for instructional cycle planning is ensuring that the knowledge and skills encompassed by proficiency scales are adequately taught. As discussed in chapter 1 (page 11), standards documents include an exorbitant amount of content per grade level or course. The process of prioritizing standards certainly helps to minimize this challenge but does not eliminate it. The processes of curriculum mapping and instructional cycle development support teachers by ensuring that they address the *most important content* adequately in the available instructional time. It is not possible to plan instruction perfectly for all students in terms of time spent on teaching standards. However, curriculum mapping and instructional cycle development certainly increase the likelihood that adequate time is allocated to teaching the most important content and that it is presented in the most logical order.

A secondary purpose for instructional cycle planning is determining the use of curriculum resources. As mentioned previously, it is common for teachers or teams of teachers to rely on textbooks or other resources when teaching academic content. Curriculum mapping and instructional cycle development identify priority standards and pacing, providing insight as to which parts of the textbook (chapters, lessons, assessments, and so on) best support instruction on the most important content. Thus, the textbook truly serves as a resource for teaching the academic content in any instructional cycle. Of course, it is not necessary to use a textbook to teach academic content. Instructional cycle planning is still helpful for teachers who are not using textbooks as their primary resource. Because the instructional cycle involves identifying the critical content to be learned for each cycle, teachers have valuable information for selecting relevant teaching resources, as they deem necessary.

With these purposes in mind, the following sections describe each of the eight steps that make up the cycle. Individual teachers can address these eight steps, but as always, we recommend that teachers work with their content-area or grade-level teams to increase quality and decrease variability.

Step 1: Identifying the Focus of the Instructional Cycle

The first step for a teacher or team of teachers is determining the focus of the instructional cycle. The source of information for this decision is the curriculum map. Consider the excerpt from a seventh-grade ELA curriculum map in figure 3.2 (page 40).

The curriculum map indicates that the focus of unit 1 is story elements and text features, which involves both literary and informational texts. The duration of unit 1 is twelve weeks, and multiple priority and supporting standards will be taught during this period of time. As mentioned on page 37, an instructional cycle is typically one to six weeks long. Since unit 1 covers twelve weeks, it is necessary to develop multiple cycles of instruction within the unit, each lasting a few weeks.

One of the priority standards in this unit concerns citing textual evidence. This information dictates that the teacher or team of teachers develops an instructional cycle for this particular topic. As part of this planning step, the teacher or team should also determine the amount of time to spend teaching the cycle. As an example, suppose that the grade 7 team determines that the citing textual evidence cycle will last fourteen to sixteen days. This decision is based on a few factors. First, the team uses previous experience as a predictor for the amount of time needed to teach the knowledge and skills included in the standards. Second, they consider the standards included in the cycle and their level of comprehensiveness and complexity. The number of priority and supporting standards to be taught affects how many days will be included in the cycle. Lastly, they determine whether the priority standards will be addressed in future instructional cycles. Additional opportunity to learn at a later time likely decreases the amount of time for the current instructional cycle.

We recommend using a template of some sort to record the results of instructional cycle planning decisions and other important information. The design of the template can be based on the preferences of the teacher or team of teachers who will be using it. We suggest keeping it simple and only including places for information that the team values and will use. While many teachers and teams of teachers find it adequate to use chart

Grade 7 Curriculum Map					
Unit and Timeline	**Unit 1** **Weeks 1–12**		**Unit 2** **Weeks 13–24**		**Unit 3** **Weeks 25–36**	
Genre	Literary and Informational		Literary and Informational		Literary and Informational	
Big Idea	Story Elements and Text Features		Author's Craft and Text Structure Research Skills and Presentations		Apply Concepts of Comprehension	
Reading Literary Standards	Priority: 7.RL.KID.1—Cite textual evidence 7.RL.KID.2—Determine theme; provide summary	Supporting: 7.RL.KID.3—Interaction of literary elements 7.RL.CAS.6—Analyze development and contrasts of points of view	Priority: 7.RL.KID.1—Cite textual evidence 7.RL.CAS.4—Figurative and connotative meanings 7.RL.IKI.9—Compare and contrast fiction to history	Supporting: 7.RL.CAS.5—Analyze structure of drama or poem 7.RL.IKI.7—Compare and contrast text to multimedia version	Priority: 7.RL.KID.2—Determine theme; objective summary 7.RL.CAS.4—Figurative and connotative meanings 7.RL.IKI.9—Compare and contrast fiction to history	Supporting: 7.RL.CAS.5—Analyze structure of drama or poem 7.RL.CAS.6—Analyze development and contrasts of points of view 7.RL.IKI.7—Compare and contrast text to multimedia version
Reading Informational Standards	Priority: 7.RI.KID.1—Cite textual evidence 7.RI.KID.2—Determine central idea; provide summary	Supporting: 7.RI.KID.3—Analyze interactions of individuals or events 7.RI.CAS.4—Figurative, connotative, and technical meanings and tone	Priority: 7.RI.KID.1—Cite textual evidence 7.RI.KID.2—Determine central idea or theme 7.RI.CAS.6—Author's point of view 7.RI.IKI.8—Trace and evaluate arguments and sound reasoning	Supporting: 7.RI.CAS.4—Figurative, connotative, and technical meanings and tone 7.RI.CAS.5—Analyze organization 7.RI.IKI.7—Compare and contrast text to multimedia 7.RI.IKI.9—Analyze multiple authors' interpretations of the same topic	Priority: 7.RI.KID.1—Cite textual evidence 7.RI.KID.2—Determine and analyze development of central ideas; provide objective summary 7.RI.CAS.6—Author's point of view 7.RI.IKI.8—Trace and evaluate arguments and sound reasoning	Supporting: 7.RI.CAS.4—Figurative, connotative, and technical meanings and tone 7.RI.CAS.5—Analyze organization 7.RI.IKI.7—Compare and contrast text to multimedia 7.RI.IKI.9—Analyze multiple authors' interpretations of the same topic

Source: © 2021 by Archdiocese of Chicago. Used with permission.
Source for standards: Archdiocese of Chicago, n.d.b.

Figure 3.2: Sample curriculum map for grade 7 ELA.

paper or an informal electronic recording document as they plan the instructional unit, "a well-organized template that captures the unit designer's thinking as the unit plan is developed can aid not only the teacher doing the design but also teachers who may review or use the unit plan later" (Heflebower et al., 2019, p. 23). While we recommend using a template, teachers and teams are the best judges of what planning tools to use in their own circumstances.

Figure 3.3 exemplifies such a template, with the work of step 1, identifying the focus of the instructional cycle, recorded. The number of the instructional cycle, its topic, and its duration appear in the first two lines of the heading. The relevant standards are recorded on the third line of the heading. Note that the priority standard is in bold in the example and supporting standards are in regular text. The remainder of the form consists of a cell for each day of instruction in the cycle, which will be used for daily lesson planning. As we progress through the eight-step instructional cycle, we will revisit this template, showing how to add appropriate content step by step until the instructional cycle is complete.

Instructional Cycle 1: Citing Textual Evidence 14 to 16 days Standards: **7.RI.KID.1**, 7.RL.CAS.6, 7.RI.CAS.4			
Day 1	Day 2	Day 3	Day 4
Day 5	Day 6	Day 7	Day 8
Day 9	Day 10	Day 11	Day 12
Day 13	Day 14	Day 15	Day 16

Source for standards: Archdiocese of Chicago, n.d.b.

Figure 3.3: Instructional cycle plan, step 1.

*Visit **MarzanoResources.com/reproducibles** for a blank reproducible version of this figure.*

Step 2: Reviewing the Relevant Standards and Proficiency Scales

Once the teacher or team of teachers has identified the focus of the instructional cycle, the next critical step is to examine the standards related to the topic of the cycle. This is to ensure that the teachers have a clear and common understanding of the knowledge and skills encompassed within the standards. At this point, it is prudent for teachers to hold a discussion about the standards. Questions relevant to this discussion include but are not limited to the following.

1. What knowledge and skills are included in the standards?

2. How have we previously taught the standards?

3. What foundational knowledge is needed prior to teaching the standards?

4. What resources do we have for teaching the standards?

5. Are there supporting standards that can be addressed as we teach the priority standards?

Sometimes the discussion about the standards included in the instructional cycle may be relatively brief. At other times, a team of teachers will spend considerable time ensuring consistent understanding of the standards. Regardless of the amount of time spent, the conversation about the individual standards included in the cycle is a helpful refresher.

It also makes sense to examine the proficiency scales related to the standards being taught in the cycle. In some cases, the teacher or teacher team participating in this process may choose to make subtle or even more significant revisions to the scales as a result of this step. For example, discussion about a proficiency scale may lead the teachers to add additional vocabulary terms to a scale. Or, they might reword a learning target on the scale in an effort to make it clearer. In some schools and districts, scale revision is a scheduled professional learning activity. When this is the case, the discussion about proficiency scales results in the teacher or team recording their suggested scale revisions for consideration during the scheduled scale revision process.

Figure 3.4 displays the citing textual evidence proficiency scale that is the focus of this instructional cycle. The target content on the scale (score 3.0) is what the teacher or team of teachers aspires for all students to master by the end of the cycle. This particular scale will be referenced throughout the remaining steps of the instructional cycle process. While there are two other standards included in this cycle, they are supporting standards and therefore not the subject of separate scales.

Grade 7 ELA
Citing Textual Evidence

7.RI.KID.1—Cite several pieces of textual evidence to support analysis of what the text says explicitly as well as inferences drawn from the text.	
Score 4.0	In addition to score 3.0, the student demonstrates in-depth inferences or application of knowledge. For example, the student will: • Analyze the quality of textual evidence used to support an inference
Score 3.0	The student will: • Cite several pieces of textual evidence that support an inference in informational text
Score 2.0	The student will: • Recognize or recall specific vocabulary, such as *claim*, *evidence*, *explicitly*, *imply*, *inference* • Cite several pieces of evidence that support what an informational text says explicitly
Score 1.0	With help, the student demonstrates knowledge of some score 2.0 and score 3.0 content.

Source for standard: Archdiocese of Chicago, n.d.b.

Figure 3.4: Proficiency scale for the citing textual evidence instructional cycle.

Additionally, this is a prime time for teachers to discuss the supports they will provide for exceptional learners and other students during the opportunities to learn the content on the proficiency scales. In order for teachers to use proficiency scales appropriately with all students, it is paramount that they understand three important terms: (1) accommodations, (2) modifications, and (3) instructional supports.

First, *accommodations* are "changes to how information is presented, how students are asked to respond, where instruction takes place, and the timing or scheduling of instruction" (Heflebower et al., 2014, p. 75). These changes are implemented to support a student in acquiring mastery of grade-level content. Because accommodations don't change the expected level of learning, a teacher can provide them to any student in the classroom. However, they are *required* for students who have been formally identified as exceptional learners (students with disabilities, English learners, or gifted and talented students). Some common accommodations include the following.

- Providing a quiet work environment

- Repeating directions or stating them in simpler words

- Providing graphic organizers to help organize a task or thinking

- Providing a technology device for recording ideas or responses to questions

- Allowing an extended amount of time for completing a task

Modifications are also supports put in place to help learners. However, they *do* change the level of learning expected of students:

> For students with disabilities or English learners, examples of common modifications include reducing the difficulty or amount of content, administering an assessment from a lower grade level, or changing the format of assessment items. For gifted and talented students, modifications would involve raising the difficulty of content and assessments. Modifications typically only apply to a small number of students. (Hoegh, 2020, p. 76)

In short, modifications are supports that shift the grade-level expectations either up or down, depending on the needs of the individual student. Accommodations and modifications will be addressed in the context of lesson planning (chapter 4, page 65).

Lastly, *instructional supports* are intended to support any and all students during the opportunity to learn. Examples of instructional supports include graphic organizers, worked examples, simplified directions, visual representations, repetition, and paraphrasing. Since the instructional supports don't change the level of expectation of any learning target on the proficiency scale, they can be provided for any and all students as the teacher deems necessary or helpful. Instructional supports are typically tightly aligned to the learning targets being addressed on the proficiency scale, while accommodations may be more general in nature. Additionally, instructional supports are not provided during assessments (unless required by an exceptional learner's individualized education program [IEP]). For exceptional learners, instructional supports are provided in addition to their accommodations or modifications.

During this step of the cycle, the teacher or team of teachers should determine instructional supports for specific learning targets on the relevant proficiency scales. To illustrate, consider the expanded proficiency scale for third-grade ELA in figure 3.5 (page 44).

Notice the added column on the right side of the scale for suggested instructional supports. The supports listed for this proficiency scale are specific to the learning targets at each score level. The score 3.0 learning target requires students to compare and contrast story elements, such as setting and plot. A student with a disability or one who simply

GRADE 3 ELA PROFICIENCY SCALE	
Priority standard: Compare and contrast the themes, settings, and plots of stories written by the same author about the same or similar characters (in books from a series, for example; RL.3.9)	
Proficiency Scale	**Instructional Supports**
4.0 To demonstrate going beyond proficiency, the student will, for example: • Compare and contrast the themes, settings, and plots of two texts using textual evidence	• Provide a bulleted list of directions for the multistep task related to this scale level.
3.5 In addition to score 3.0, in-depth inferences and applications with partial success	
3.0 The student will: • Compare and contrast the themes, settings, and plots of stories written by the same author about the same or similar characters	• Provide a T-chart graphic organizer for comparing and contrasting the themes, settings, and plots of a story. • Provide sample language for students to draw on as they complete the compare and contrast activity. • Chunk the compare and contrast activity into smaller parts, giving directions and information for each part when relevant.
2.5 No major errors or omissions regarding 2.0 content and partial knowledge of the 3.0 content	
2.0 The student will recognize or recall specific vocabulary, such as *compare, contrast, plot, theme.* The student will perform basic processes, such as: • Identify simple themes and plots in stories • Identify the setting of a story	• Discuss themes, plots, and settings from previously read stories to activate background knowledge. • Provide a vocabulary organizer for the student to record word descriptions to draw on throughout the learning opportunity.
1.5 Partial knowledge of the 2.0 content but major errors or omissions regarding the 3.0 content	
1.0 With help, a partial understanding of some 2.0 content (the simpler details and processes) and some 3.0 content (the more complex ideas and processes)	

Source for standard: NGA & CCSSO, 2010a.

Figure 3.5: Grade 3 ELA proficiency scale with instructional supports.

struggles with this task is more likely to succeed if the teacher provides a graphic organizer for completing the comparison. This instructional support doesn't decrease the expectations of the standard; it simply provides additional support to the student as he or she strives to learn the academic content and ultimately demonstrate mastery of the standard.

Clearly, adding instructional supports to the proficiency scale requires thought, expertise, and time on the part of the teachers providing the learning opportunity. However, it is well worth the effort when the instructional supports assist students in moving up the scale and demonstrating growth over time. It is important to note that determining appropriate instructional supports can occur in an ongoing manner throughout the instructional cycle. By including consideration of instructional supports at this stage, you ensure it becomes a regular part of the instructional planning process.

Step 3: Planning to Collect Evidence of Student Learning

Step 3 involves deciding on assessments that you will administer during the instructional cycle. This includes preassessments, checks for understanding, and end-of-cycle assessments. Again, this may be the effort of an individual teacher or a team of teachers working together to plan the cycle. Regardless, it is important to plan assessments *before* teaching begins, as assessment data inform further instruction. Assessments are how you know whether students are learning the knowledge and skills set forth in the proficiency scales. Therefore, teachers, whether working individually or in a team, must determine the assessments that they will use to collect evidence about what students know at specific points during the unit. Figure 3.6 modifies the instructional cycle template initially shown in figure 3.3 (page 41) by adding planned assessments on appropriate days over the course of the unit.

Instructional Cycle 1: Citing Textual Evidence 14 to 16 days Standards: **7.RI.KID.1**, 7.RL.CAS.6, 7.RI.CAS.4			
Day 1	**Day 2**	**Day 3**	**Day 4**
Citing Textual Evidence Preassessment			Check for Understanding 1
Day 5	**Day 6**	**Day 7**	**Day 8**
		Check for Understanding 2	
Day 9	**Day 10**	**Day 11**	**Day 12**
	Check for Understanding 3		
Day 13	**Day 14**	**Day 15**	**Day 16**
Citing Textual Evidence End-of-Cycle Assessment			

Source for standards: Archdiocese of Chicago, n.d.b.

Figure 3.6: Instructional cycle plan, step 3.

In figure 3.6, the teacher or team of teachers has decided to include a preassessment on the first day of the cycle. The intent of this assessment is to discover the amount of background knowledge students have about citing textual evidence in an informational text.

The more background knowledge students have, the less time a teacher needs to spend teaching score 2.0 content. Sometimes a preassessment results in differentiated instruction early in the cycle to better meet the needs of all learners. For example, if the preassessment discloses that only a few students need support with the academic vocabulary presented on the scale, the teacher may provide these students with explicit instruction related to the vocabulary. The rest of the class will not receive this vocabulary instruction. Even if you do not differentiate at this point, preassessment data can inform you about which students to monitor more closely as the cycle evolves.

Days 4, 7, and 10 of the cycle each include a check for understanding. These periodic assessments are administered to ensure that students are showing gradual growth as the learning opportunity progresses. Checks for understanding are typically brief assessments. They often focus on a single learning target from the proficiency scale or perhaps a single score level. For example, early in the cycle, a teacher might offer students a check for understanding that covers the score 2.0 learning targets on the proficiency scale. Checks for understanding might involve informal assessments, such as partner discussions or exit slips. They can also be more formal, like a quiz. It is common for multiple checks for understanding to occur throughout the instructional cycle. Again, a significant benefit of periodic assessments is that the information gleaned helps to inform the instruction that follows.

On day 13, the teacher will administer an end-of-cycle assessment, encompassing the knowledge and skills learned on days 1 through 12 of the cycle. Teachers will typically administer an end-of-cycle assessment after students have received instruction on all the learning targets for that unit, but before the very end of the instructional cycle. (The last few days of the cycle provide time for extension and remediation.) This is often an assessment designed by a single classroom teacher, but it might also be one designed by a team of teachers that teach the same course or grade level and are using the same set of identified priority standards and proficiency scales. When a team of teachers creates and administers the same assessment, it is referred to as a *common assessment*. While some teacher teams might share all their assessments, the end-of-cycle assessment especially is most often created, administered, and analyzed collaboratively in an effort to effectively plan how to support students based on the data. We provide additional detail about standards-based assessments in chapter 5 (page 91).

Step 4: Writing a SMART Goal

Step 4 is the last step of the cycle that occurs prior to actually teaching the knowledge and skills on the proficiency scale or scales. At this point, the teacher or team of teachers crafts a SMART goal for the unit. A SMART goal is one that is strategic and specific, measurable, attainable, results-oriented, and time-bound (Conzemius & O'Neill, 2014). Standards-based tools like proficiency scales and aligned assessments enable teachers to track student learning by setting goals for class achievement and growth and monitoring progress toward those goals.

Since an instructional cycle is based on a proficiency scale or small set of related scales, the SMART goal should refer to desired student performance on the scale at the end of the cycle. The following example shows a SMART goal that a teacher or team of teachers might come up with in this step for the citing textual evidence cycle: By the end of the cycle for citing textual evidence, 75 percent of students will demonstrate mastery of the priority standard, with all students demonstrating growth.

This SMART goal is specific to this instructional cycle focused on citing textual evidence. The percentage of students reaching mastery makes it measurable. The team of teachers determined the percentage; therefore, it can be assumed that the team deems the goal attainable. Clearly, the goal is results-oriented, as evidenced by the phrase "demonstrate mastery." Finally, the duration of time for the instructional cycle—fourteen to sixteen days—ensures that the goal is time-bound.

The goal percentage of students achieving mastery (in this case, 75 percent) may vary from cycle to cycle. For example, a SMART goal for a different cycle might aim for 50 percent as the degree of mastery desired. A lower percentage goal such as this could be a function of the newness of the content for the students in the grade level or course. Or, teachers might set a lower percentage goal if the scale will be addressed again in future instructional cycles. Conversely, a SMART goal might include a higher percentage if the content has previously been taught. This target will not be the same every time; instead, the educators setting the goal aim for a percentage that is attainable, but also creates a sense of urgency regarding the instructional time allocated.

You may be wondering why the SMART goal for this cycle doesn't require 100 percent of students to attain mastery. There are multiple reasons for this, including the following.

1. The standard may be addressed again in a later cycle of instruction, at which point additional students will attain mastery.

2. Time for reteaching and reinforcement is built into the cycle following the end-of-cycle assessment (described in step 8). Therefore, if the goal is not met on the end-of-cycle assessment, additional time is available to support students and ultimately meet the goal.

3. The language of the SMART goal also includes "all students demonstrating growth." Some students may not attain mastery of the score 3.0 knowledge and skills by the end of the cycle. However, if they move up on the scale from where they began at the beginning of the cycle, it can be acknowledged as success.

The fact that the SMART goal is based on a cycle of instruction means that it is also time sensitive. We view this as a positive feature because a teacher or team of teachers is able to ascertain whether they have reached their goal in a relatively short period of time, depending on the length of the instructional cycle. Additionally, time-sensitive goals focused on student learning can foster a culture of collective responsibility and help teams concentrate on student growth over time more effectively (Marzano et al., 2016).

Figure 3.7 (page 48) shows the instructional cycle template once again. Notice the inclusion of the SMART goal as a result of step 4.

Instructional Cycle 1: Citing Textual Evidence			
14 to 16 days			
Standards: **7.RI.KID.1**, 7.RL.CAS.6, 7.RI.CAS.4			
SMART goal: By the end of the cycle for citing textual evidence, 75 percent of students will demonstrate mastery of the priority standard, with all students demonstrating growth.			
Day 1	**Day 2**	**Day 3**	**Day 4**
Citing Textual Evidence Preassessment			Check for Understanding 1
Day 5	**Day 6**	**Day 7**	**Day 8**
		Check for Understanding 2	
Day 9	**Day 10**	**Day 11**	**Day 12**
	Check for Understanding 3		
Day 13	**Day 14**	**Day 15**	**Day 16**
Citing Textual Evidence End-of-Cycle Assessment			

Source for standards: Archdiocese of Chicago, n.d.b.

Figure 3.7: Instructional cycle plan, step 4.

Step 5: Planning and Teaching Daily Lessons Within the Cycle

With steps 1 through 4 complete, it is now time to plan for the daily lessons that will transmit the knowledge and skills from the proficiency scale to students. While it is definitely possible to plan the daily instruction for the entire cycle prior to actually teaching it, a teacher or team of teachers must embrace the idea that daily lesson planning is a fluid process. In *The New Art and Science of Teaching*, Marzano (2017) shared this idea:

> I believe it is an ineffective practice to plan one lesson at a time. Instead, teachers should plan from the perspective of the unit, which should provide an overarching framework for instruction. I like to refer to this initial plan as a *draft unit plan*. This name helps communicate the fact that a unit of instruction is always a work in progress. (p. 107)

Indeed, instruction must be a fluid process, as the results of each assessment opportunity have the potential to change any existing instructional plans. In fact, it is prudent to consider each assessment opportunity as a checkpoint for a cluster of daily lessons. In other words, the daily lessons prepare students for the specific assessment opportunity, which in turn informs the next few lessons.

The main idea of this step in the instructional cycle is that teachers plan day-to-day instruction. Since the instructional cycle is based on a proficiency scale or multiple related proficiency scales, the foundational knowledge will be the subject of lessons early in the cycle. This includes the vocabulary that students need to know, as well as the other foundational knowledge represented at score 2.0 on the proficiency scales. As the cycle progresses, the daily lessons address the target content at score 3.0. We will address designing and teaching individual lessons in much more detail in chapter 4 (page 65).

When teachers work in teams to plan instructional cycles, some teams collaboratively plan the day-to-day opportunities to learn, resulting in very similar lessons delivered across classrooms. Other teams choose for individual teachers to plan independently. When this occurs, teachers employ the same standards and overall unit plan, but allow for variance in how they teach the content. Either approach is fine, as long as the end result is students learning the priority standards.

Figure 3.8 (page 50) continues to expand the citing textual evidence unit plan displayed previously. Daily lesson plans are embedded within the instructional cycle. Here, lesson plans are identified by number as a placeholder; specific topics will be filled in when we discuss lesson planning in chapter 4 (page 65). Lessons 1 through 3 provide the opportunity to learn the knowledge and skills that will be assessed on Check for Understanding 1. Lessons 4 through 6 will provide learning opportunities in preparation for Check for Understanding 2, and so on. The end-of-cycle assessment or common assessment typically includes items and tasks that address all levels of the proficiency scale with the heaviest focus on the score 3.0 content. This type of daily lesson planning requires teachers to consider instruction and assessment as interdependent components within the instructional cycle: lessons inform assessments and assessment results inform further lessons.

One last important thought regarding this step in the instructional cycle process is in relation to the supporting standards. While the supporting standards are typically not formally assessed, they may be taught explicitly during the cycle. Sometimes the knowledge and skills encompassed within the supporting standards are also embedded within the opportunity to learn the knowledge and skills included in the priority standard. While the supporting standards don't receive the same amount of instructional focus as the priority standards, teachers should make every effort to ensure students have a chance to master these supplementary topics as well. That is, it is important to include the supporting standards in your planning for the instructional cycle as well.

Step 6: Administering and Scoring the End-of-Cycle Assessment

After you have taught each of your daily lesson plans (see chapter 4, page 65, for more detail), it is time to administer the end-of-cycle assessment. The primary purpose for this assessment is to collect data that indicate how each student is performing on the proficiency scales included in the cycle. The teacher or team of teachers examines these data, which guide the instructional planning for the remainder of the cycle.

Of course, if you are planning and executing the instructional cycle as part of a team, the end-of-cycle assessment is likely a common assessment. When multiple teachers are giving their classes a common assessment, they have a discussion prior to administering the assessment to ensure similar practices. For example, all teachers involved need to either allow students to read the directions on their own or read the directions to them. The goal of a team of teachers regarding common assessment administration is to give the test as uniformly as possible.

Instructional Cycle 1: Citing Textual Evidence 14 to 16 days Standards: **7.RI.KID.1**, 7.RL.CAS.6, 7.RI.CAS.4			
SMART goal: By the end of the cycle for citing textual evidence, 75 percent of students will demonstrate mastery of the priority standard, with all students demonstrating growth.			
Day 1	**Day 2**	**Day 3**	**Day 4**
Citing Textual Evidence Preassessment Daily Lesson Plan 1	Daily Lesson Plan 2	Daily Lesson Plan 3	Check for Understanding 1 Daily Lesson Plan 4
Day 5	**Day 6**	**Day 7**	**Day 8**
Daily Lesson Plan 5	Daily Lesson Plan 6	Check for Understanding 2 Daily Lesson Plan 7	Daily Lesson Plan 8
Day 9	**Day 10**	**Day 11**	**Day 12**
Daily Lesson Plan 9	Check for Understanding 3 Daily Lesson Plan 10	Daily Lesson Plan 11	Daily Lesson Plan 12
Day 13	**Day 14**	**Day 15**	**Day 16**
Citing Textual Evidence End-of-Cycle Assessment	Daily Lesson Plan 14	Daily Lesson Plan 15	Daily Lesson Plan 16

Source for standards: Archdiocese of Chicago, n.d.b.

Figure 3.8: Instructional cycle plan, step 5.

Once students have taken the common or end-of-cycle assessment, it is time to attend to the scoring process. Teachers' end goal of the scoring process is to ascertain students' performance levels based on the proficiency scales covered on the end-of-cycle assessment. This is true whether a single teacher is involved in the instructional cycle process or a team of teachers. When it is a team of teachers scoring the assessment, it is very important that they use an agreed-on set of scoring guidelines to ensure that they make consistent scoring decisions. As previously stated, teachers will use the results of the end-of-cycle assessments to determine next steps for instruction within the cycle.

Step 7: Implementing the Assessment Data Protocol

After scoring students' end-of-cycle assessments or common assessments, the next step is to examine the overall results. Recall the SMART goal established in step 4 of the cycle. Now is the time when individual teachers or teams can discover whether they have met their goal. To do so, we recommend using an assessment data protocol.

An assessment data protocol typically includes a set of four or five questions about the results of the assessment, as well as a few action steps for teachers to take based on the answers to the questions. Teachers or teams can create their own protocols to best serve their purposes, but we recommend the following questions.

1. On which parts of the assessment did students perform well? Why do we believe this is the case?

2. On which parts of the assessment did students struggle? Why do we believe this is the case?

3. Do we need to revise any assessment items? Which items? Why?

4. Which students are in need of special attention?

5. Are there other important findings about this assessment that we need to record?

By answering the questions within the protocol, a teacher or team of teachers can determine action steps related to the assessment or instruction. For example, the data may suggest that a specific assessment item is confusing and needs revising. Or the data may disclose that a subset of students needs instructional support on the foundational knowledge and skills. Instructional planning can occur to address this need. The primary purpose for the protocol is to inform next steps for the teachers.

Figure 3.9 (page 52) is a sample team assessment data protocol. Notice that the SMART goal and its results are recorded at the top of the figure (the percentage of students who reached score 3.0 and the percentage who demonstrated growth). The students who comprise the 72 percent mastery met the requirements of score 3.0 performance per the end-of-cycle assessment. The students included in the 95 percent growth moved up on the proficiency scale from where they performed at the beginning of the cycle. The teachers answered each question in relation to a common assessment for the citing textual evidence instructional cycle.

Although this protocol is designed for use by a team of teachers working with a common assessment, the questions can be adapted and used by an individual teacher reviewing an assessment she designed and gave in her own classroom. While the data set will be restricted to just her students, the process of analysis will still provide important insights into the progress of her students and the quality of the assessment she developed.

This type of data examination takes time, but it creates the potential for student performance to reach high levels. When teachers know how students are performing on a proficiency scale, it gives them insight to next steps for instruction, as well as revisions needed to improve the quality of the assessment.

Step 8: Providing Support for All Learners

The final step in the instructional cycle is differentiated support for all learners based on the results of the end-of-cycle or common assessment, as analyzed through the assessment data protocol. The fourth question in the assessment data protocol asks the teacher or team of teachers to identify students who require special attention. More specifically, *special attention* means reteaching, reinforcement, and enrichment. This means that some students (those who score lower on the scale) will receive additional opportunities to learn the content taught earlier in the citing textual evidence cycle, while others who are proficient receive further practicing and deepening opportunities. There are also students who have reached an advanced level with the content and need enrichment activities.

Assessment Data Protocol	Instructional Cycle 1 Citing Textual Evidence		
SMART goal: By the end of the cycle for citing textual evidence, 75 percent of students will demonstrate mastery of the priority standard, with all students demonstrating growth. SMART goal results: 72 percent mastery, 95 percent growth			
1. On which parts of the assessment did students perform well? Why do we believe this is the case?	• Students did well on the score 2.0 items on the assessment. We spent three or four class periods addressing the foundational knowledge and skills, and it apparently paid off. • The majority of students did well on the first and second score 3.0 items. These were the easier items, as responses were based on information stated explicitly within the text.		
2. On which parts of the assessment did students struggle? Why do we believe this is the case?	• A good number of students struggled on the score 3.0 extended-response item. It is a challenging item in that it requires students to respond to multiple components as well as make an inference.		
3. Do we need to revise any assessment items? Which items? Why?	• Test Item #3—We need to come up with different wording for option *d* on this selected-response question because it stands out as significantly different from options *a*, *b*, and *c*. • Test Item #8—We must reformat this question to emphasize the multiple components students are required to answer.		
4. Which students are in need of special attention?	Additional opportunity to learn: Calvin Leon Ashley Sharika Tyrone Austin	Additional practicing and deepening: All students not listed in other columns	Enrichment: Abby Nate Leni Logan Kyle Tammy Jeff Keegan Lily Paulo Liliana
5. Are there other important findings about this assessment that we need to record?	• It took some students quite a bit of time to complete. We might consider breaking the administration into two class periods or decreasing the number of items on the assessment in order to address this.		
Action steps resulting from the data:	1. Revise assessment items as indicated in response to protocol question 3. 2. Plan intervention based on the answer to question 4. 3. Discuss changing assessment administration guidance based on response to protocol question 5.		

Source: Adapted from Marzano et al., 2016.

Figure 3.9: Assessment data protocol.

*Visit **MarzanoResources.com/reproducibles** for a blank reproducible version of this figure.*

All three scenarios are based on the results of the end-of-cycle assessment. The number of days allocated for this important differentiation was determined in step 1 of the cycle. However, the teacher or team can make adjustments at this stage based on how well students acquire the knowledge and skills on the relevant proficiency scales. For example, if students collectively perform well on the end-of-cycle assessment, the teacher may determine that moving into the next cycle early is appropriate. Alternatively, student performance may indicate that an additional day for intervention is needed. When this is the case, it is important to remember that extending the current cycle impacts the amount of time available for the next cycle. Therefore, we recommend following the number of days allocated for each cycle whenever possible.

Figure 3.10 (page 54) once again displays the instructional cycle plan for citing textual evidence, with plans for the days following the end-of-cycle assessment. Notice that day 14 now includes a writing activity. On the day after administering the end-of-cycle assessment, the teacher is likely still scoring the assessment and planning for reteaching, reinforcing, and enrichment. There are various activities that can occur on this day to continue instruction while providing the teacher the time needed to prepare for supporting all students based on the assessment data. For example, the teacher might conduct a mini-unit that addresses a supporting standard or two, or continue core instruction related to the priority standards, especially if he or she suspects that the SMART goal has not been met.

Days 15 and 16 are dedicated to providing instruction that will improve student performance based on the assessment data. There are various ways these days can be organized. For example, a team of three teachers can divide the students into flexible groups based on question 4 of the assessment data protocol. In this case, one teacher plans instruction for students that need additional opportunities to learn, another plans for reinforcement of the content, while the third teacher plans for two days of enrichment. If one of the groups is too large for one teacher to manage, another educator such as a special education teacher, para-educator, building leader, or instructional coach can come in to assist. The goal is for the students in each group to receive instruction based on their needs. An individual teacher can use this same strategy by enlisting the support of other adults in the building for the days when intervention is provided. Or, he or she may choose to set up the classroom such that small-group instruction occurs while the other students engage in structured independent activities.

The eight steps of the instructional cycle are intended to increase the likelihood that students are successful in learning important academic content. They are designed to provide a logical, informative, and effective process whether it is one teacher providing the learning opportunities or a team of teachers.

Instructional Cycle 1: Citing Textual Evidence			
14 to 16 days			
Standards: **7.RI.KID.1**, 7.RL.CAS.6, 7.RI.CAS.4			
SMART goal: By the end of the cycle for citing textual evidence, 75 percent of students will demonstrate mastery of the priority standard, with all students demonstrating growth.			
Day 1	**Day 2**	**Day 3**	**Day 4**
Citing Textual Evidence Preassessment Daily Lesson Plan 1	Daily Lesson Plan 2	Daily Lesson Plan 3	Check for Understanding 1 Daily Lesson Plan 4
Day 5	**Day 6**	**Day 7**	**Day 8**
Daily Lesson Plan 5	Daily Lesson Plan 6	Check for Understanding 2 Daily Lesson Plan 7	Daily Lesson Plan 8
Day 9	**Day 10**	**Day 11**	**Day 12**
Daily Lesson Plan 9	Check for Understanding 3 Daily Lesson Plan 10	Daily Lesson Plan 11	Daily Lesson Plan 12
Day 13	**Day 14**	**Day 15**	**Day 16**
Citing Textual Evidence End-of-Cycle Assessment	Daily Lesson Plan 14 Writing Activity	Daily Lesson Plan 15 Reteaching, Reinforcement, Enrichment	Daily Lesson Plan 16 Reteaching, Reinforcement, Enrichment

Source for standards: Archdiocese of Chicago, n.d.b.

Figure 3.10: Instructional cycle plan, step 8.

Sample Instructional Cycle Plans

Now that we've described each of the eight steps of the instructional cycle, this section shares a few additional examples of instructional cycle plans.

Figure 3.11 displays an instructional cycle developed by a team of first-grade teachers. They have chosen to use a team-developed template for each cycle within the first-grade academic year. Each step in the instructional cycle is represented in the template, including the cycle's proficiency scales and specific information about daily lesson planning and assessment.

Grade: 1	Quarter Taught: Third
Unit: Halves and Wholes	Duration of Unit: 6–8 class periods

SMART Goal for the Cycle:

By the end of the cycle for halves and wholes, 80 percent of students will demonstrate mastery of the standards included in the cycle.

Grade-Level Priority Standards:

- Standard: 1.G.3—
  a. Partition circles and rectangles into two equal shares.
  b. Describe the shares using the word *halves* and the phrase *half of*.
  c. Describe the whole as two of the shares.
- Standard: 1.MD.3—Tell and write time to the hour and half hour (including using the terms *o'clock* and *half past*) using analog and digital clocks.

Supporting Standards:

- 1.G.1—Distinguish between defining attributes versus nondefining attributes. Use defining attributes to build and draw two-dimensional shapes.
- 1.G.2—Compose a new shape or solid from two-dimensional shapes or three-dimensional solids.

Previous Grade-Level Standards:	Grade-Level Standards:	Next Grade-Level Standards:

• K.G.1—Describe objects in the environment using names of shapes and solids (squares, circles, triangles, rectangles, cubes, and spheres).
 	
• K.G.2—Correctly name shapes and solids (squares, circles, triangles, rectangles, cubes, and spheres) regardless of their orientations or overall sizes.
	• 1.G.3—
	  a. Partition circles and rectangles into two equal shares.
	  b. Describe the shares using the word *halves* and the phrase *half of*.
	  c. Describe the whole as two of the shares.
	• 1.MD.3—Tell and write time to the hour and half hour (including using the terms *o'clock* and *half past*) using analog and digital clocks.
		• 2.G.2—Partition a rectangle into rows and columns of same-size squares and count to find the total number.
		
		• 2.G.3—Partition circles and rectangles into two, three, or four equal shares. Describe the shares using the words *halves*, *thirds*, *half of*, *a third of*, and so on, and describe the whole as two halves, three thirds, or four fourths. Recognize that identical wholes can be equally divided in different ways. Demonstrate understanding that partitioning shapes into more equal shares creates smaller shares.
		
		• 2.MD.7—Tell and write time to the nearest five minutes (including quarter after and quarter to) with a.m. and p.m. using analog and digital clocks.

Halves and Wholes Proficiency Scale	
Score 4.0	In addition to score 3.0 performance, the student demonstrates in-depth inferences and applications that go beyond what was taught. For example, the student: • 1.G.3—Explores multiple ways to divide a variety of shapes into equal shares • 1.MD.3—Explores four equal shares on the clock and tells time to the fifteen-minute interval (halving and halving again)

Score 3.0	The student:
	
	• 1.G.3—
	  a. Partitions circles and rectangles into two equal shares
	  b. Describes the shares using the word *halves* and the phrase *half of*
	  c. Describes the whole as two of the shares
	• 1.MD.3—Tells and writes time to the hour and half hour (including using the terms *o'clock* and *half past*) using analog and digital clocks

Figure 3.11: Sample instructional cycle plan, grade 1 mathematics.

continued →

Score 2.0	The student recognizes or recalls specific vocabulary, such as: • *half*, *halves*, *whole*, *divide*, *equal shares*, *hour*, *half hour*, *o'clock*, *half past*, _____-*thirty*, *analog*, *digital*, *minutes*, *hour*, *minute hand*, *hour hand* The student performs basic processes, such as: • 1.G.3—Identifies a circle and a rectangle • 1.MD.3—Skip counts by fives to sixty (second-grade standard but important for teaching why the *6* on the clock is the "thirty" and the *12* on the clock makes the "whole" at sixty minutes)

Daily Lesson Plans

	Daily Lesson Activities	Assessment and Evidence	Supporting Resources
Day 1	• Present and explain the proficiency scale for the unit. • Introduce the topic of the unit as "Halves and Wholes"; activate background knowledge through discussion. • Preassess learners on score 2.0 and 3.0 content. • Provide direct instruction on key vocabulary terms (shapes) learned in kindergarten. • Revisit the rectangle and explore the concept of equal shares through a paper-folding activity. Is there more than one way to create equal shares with a rectangle? Can equal shares be made with a circle? Provide paper circles of varying sizes.	• Preassessment on score 2.0 and 3.0 content (formal)	• Shape manipulatives or paper shapes • Colored paper for paper-folding activity
Day 2	• Review of day one activity. Transfer this practice to cutting of shapes and drawing of the half-lines on rectangles and circles. • Introduce *halves* and *half of*. • Introduce *the whole*.		• Colored paper for paper-folding and cutting activity • Half-whole worksheet
Day 3	• Practice drawing rectangles and circles and then creating equal shares to identify halves and wholes. • Experiment with putting two half circles together and two squares together to create circles and rectangles (new wholes). • Use these constructing and deconstructing activities to solidify students' use of the language around fractional parts and the whole.	• Check for understanding #1 (individual student probing discussions)	• Half-circle and half-square manipulatives • Individual student practice bags

Day 4	• Review skip counting by fives to sixty. Ask students to practice with a partner. • Introduce the analog clock face. Demonstrate counting of the minutes by ones and then fives. Practice counting minutes by fives around the clock. • Explain that in place of *60*, we use the phrase *o'clock*. On the active board, show 4:00 on the analog clock and introduce the digital representation for that same time. Repeat with additional times. • Assign telling time worksheet.	• Check for understanding #2 (partner skip counting)	• Active board
Day 5	• Review skip counting by fives to sixty. • Using clock manipulatives and whiteboards, students practice making *o'clock* times in analog and digital forms. Partway through, modify the activity to be a partner task. One partner creates the analog version and the other creates the digital version; partners then check each other's work. • Assign students to stations for small-group practice. • Administer common assessment after station practice.	• District common assessment	• Station activity bags

Instructional Support Ideas

Instructional supports	Provide clock manipulatives in addition to clock images on paper. Consider large-faced clocks for easier skip counting of five-minute intervals and minute hand manipulation.

Anticipated misconceptions	• Unequal parts may be common when first dividing. Intermix the term *fair shares* with *equal shares*. Young students understand the concept of what's fair and what's not.
	
	• Students struggling with one-to-one correspondence may struggle with tracking while skip counting the minutes by fives. Using a large-printed clock face on paper allows the students to slash through each number as they say, "Five, ten, fifteen . . ."
	
	• Students often mix up the hour and minute hands.
	
	    – Teach students that the short word *hour* is the shorter hand on the clock. The longer word, *minute*, is the longer minute hand.
	
	    – Color-code hour- and minute-hand labels with the hands on the clock.
	
	    – Sing to the tune of "I'm a Little Teapot." "I'm a smaller hour hand, short and stout. I tell the hour and give a shout. I'm a longer minute hand, big and tall. I tell the minute and that's all."

continued ➡

Reteaching strategies	• Provide a large circle (hula hoop or gym floor center circle) for real-life applications and large-scale halving.
	• Introduce online games.
	• Layer the parts to see if they truly are equal. Stack the two halves of the rectangle to prove "fair shares."
Reassessment strategies	Interview students one on one to determine the level to which they can use the vocabulary and perform the skills.

Enrichment and Extension Ideas
• Error analysis on worked examples
• See level 4 on the correlating proficiency scales

Additional Information
• Components of these standards are likely to be represented in other instructional units.
• Further clarifications about the knowledge and skills included within this instructional unit:
– 1.MD.3—Skip counting by fives to sixty. (This is a level 2 expectation that is a second-grade standard, but important for teaching why the *6* on the clock is the "thirty" and the *12* on the clock makes the "whole" at sixty minutes.)
• The common assessment will be given on day five of the instructional cycle. Reteaching, reinforcement, and enrichment will occur for the next two days, based on the results of the common assessment.

Source: © 2021 by North Dakota Standards Professional Learning Grant Project. Adapted with permission.
Source for standards: North Dakota Department of Public Instruction, 2017.

The example in figure 3.12 is a high school algebra 1 instructional cycle. This team of teachers used a digital template and kept it quite simple by creating hyperlinks to various related documents, including their daily lesson plans. These hyperlinks are represented in the figure by the underlined text in the Instructional Resources and Assessments columns. As a result, this example appears much less detailed, but additional information appears in the linked files. This instructional cycle is different from the elementary example in figure 3.11 and the simple grid used in this chapter's primary example, but all three of these approaches are effective for instructional cycle planning.

A final example is from a grade 11–12 ELA unit. This team uses a proficiency scale (figure 3.13, page 60), a student tracking form listing the seven learning targets for the cycle (figure 3.14, page 61), and the instructional cycle plan (figure 3.15, page 61). Here again, resources for the instructional cycle plan, including common formative assessments (CFAs), are linked in the daily lesson sequence of the plan. The result is a very simplified but clear sequence of the twelve days of the unit, focused on major themes in American literature.

Instructional Cycle 2 Linear Functions			
Pacing	Standards	Instructional Resources	Assessments
15–18 days	• A-CED.2: Create equations in two or more variables to represent relationships between quantities; graph equations on coordinate axes with labels and scales. • F-IF.7a: Graph linear and quadratic functions and show intercepts, maxima, and minima. • F-IF.9: Compare properties of two functions each represented in a different way (algebraically, graphically, numerically in tables, or by verbal descriptions). • F-LE.2: Construct linear and exponential functions, including arithmetic and geometric sequences, given a graph, a description of a relationship, or two input-output pairs (include reading these from a table). • S-ID.7: Interpret the slope (rate of change) and the intercept (constant term) of a linear model in the context of the data; interpolate and extrapolate the linear model to predict values.	• Algebra I Pacing Guide • Linear Function Proficiency Scale • Vocabulary Matching Activity • Exit Slip 1 • Exit Slip 2 • Exit Slip 3 • Exit Slip 4 • Daily Lesson Plans	• Check for Understanding 1 • Checking for Understanding 2 • Check for Understanding 3 • Check for Understanding 4 • Mid-Unit Common Assessment • End-of-Unit Common Assessment

Source for standards: NGA & CCSSO, 2010b.

Figure 3.12: Sample instructional cycle plan, algebra 1.

Course: English				Grade: 11–12	

Standard RL.11–12.9: Demonstrate knowledge of eighteenth-, nineteenth, and early-twentieth-century foundational works of American literature, including how two or more texts from the same period treat similar themes or topics.

	Learning Targets	**CFA Score 1**	**CFA Score 2**	**CFA Score 3**
Score 4.0	**Advanced Level Performance** Students will . . . • Go beyond what is taught to make connections at a higher level, possibly including: – Explaining how a theme changes over time across multiple texts and eras – A project, presentation, or original work that draws on the source material but presents it in a new way – Combining knowledge of more than one source, or more than one subject area, to create an original, integrated work			
Score 3.5	In addition to score 3.0 performance, partial success at score 4.0 content			
Score 3.0	**Proficient Level Performance** Students will . . . a. Identify themes and topics from multiple texts b. Explain how a theme or topic is similar across multiple texts c. Explain how a theme or topic is different across multiple texts			
Score 2.5	No major errors or omissions regarding score 2.0 content, and partial success at score 3.0 content			
Score 2.0	**Basic Learning Progression Performance** Students will . . . a. Define the following vocabulary words: *eighteenth century, nineteenth century, twentieth century, foundational, theme, topic* b. Summarize the text directly, including identifying a theme or main topic c. Identify which foundational works belong to the eighteenth, nineteenth, and twentieth centuries			
Score 1.5	Partial success at score 2.0 content, and major errors or omissions regarding score 3.0 content			
Score 1.0	With help, partial success at score 2.0 content and score 3.0 content			

Source: © 2021 by Uinta County School District #1. Used with permission.
Source for standard: NGA & CCSSO, 2010a.

Figure 3.13: Proficiency scale, grade 11–12 ELA.

Student Tracker				
Standard RL.11–12.9: Demonstrate knowledge of eighteenth-, nineteenth, and early-twentieth-century foundational works of American literature, including how two or more texts from the same period treat similar themes or topics.				
Target	1	2	3	4
T1: What is the theme of the text?				
T2: How is a theme treated similarly across multiple texts?				
T3: How is a theme treated differently across multiple texts?				
T4: How does a theme change across multiple texts and time periods?				
T5: Vocabulary				
T6: Summarize a text				
T7: Correctly identify the time period of a text (18th, 19th, or 20th century)				
CFA 1: Christian Charity				
CFA 2: American Jezebel				
CFA 3: Charity & Jezebel				
Key: 1 = I don't understand this; I need the teacher's help! 2 = I kinda get it; I can do it with a group, or sometimes on my own. 3 = I get it; I can do this independently when asked. 4 = I understand this well enough to teach it, and I can apply this to new situations or texts.				

Source: © 2021 by Uinta County School District #1. Used with permission.
Source for standard: NGA & CCSSO, 2010a.

Figure 3.14: Student tracking form, grade 11–12 ELA.

Day One: Terms and Eras	Day Two: A Model of Christian Charity	Day Three: AMoCC	Day Four: First Assessment
• Bell Ringer • T5: Review vocabulary • Vocab Activity • T7: Review eras • Timeline Review Activity • Read: "A Model of Christian Charity" (AMoCC) • Grammar instruction • Sustained silent reading	• Bell Ringer • T7: Which era? • T6: Summarize the text • Answer Think and Focus questions for AMoCC • Sustained silent reading	• Bell Ringer • T1: What is one theme of the text? • Cite evidence for support • Rinse and repeat for other themes • Rewrite AMoCC into 10 words • Sustained silent reading	• CFA 1: Christian Charity • Work on presentation for next week: Create an original work that draws on the source material but presents it in a new way. • T4: Suppose you could establish a "city on a hill" like the Puritans did. Create a representation of your utopian society. How does your utopia both mirror and reflect Puritan society?

Figure 3.15: Sample instructional cycle plan, grade 11–12 ELA.

continued →

Day Five: American Jezebel	Day Six: Jezebel Discussion	Day Seven: Comparison	Day Eight: Second Assessment
• Bell Ringer • Read: "American Jezebel" (AJ) • T7: Which era? • T6: Summarize the text • Answer the Think and Focus questions for AJ • Work on utopia presentation • Grammar instruction • Sustained silent reading	• Bell Ringer • T1: What is one theme of the text? • Cite evidence for support • Rinse and repeat for other themes • Rewrite AJ into ten words • Work on utopia presentation • Sustained silent reading	• Bell Ringer • T2 & T3: Comparison activity • Discuss similarities • Discuss differences • Why do these similarities and differences exist? • Work on utopia presentation • Sustained silent reading	• CFA 2: American Jezebel • Presentations: Create an original work that draws on the source material but presents it in a new way. • T4: Suppose you could establish a "city on a hill" like the Puritans did. Create a representation of your utopian society. How does your utopia both mirror and reflect Puritan society?
Day Nine: To My Dear and Loving Husband	Day Ten: To My Dear and Loving Husband	Day Eleven: Comparison	Day Twelve: Third Assessment
• Bell Ringer • Read: "To My Dear and Loving Husband" (TMDLH) • T7: Which era? • T6: Summarize the text • Answer Think and Focus questions for TMDLH • Grammar instruction • Sustained silent reading	• Bell Ringer • T1: What is one theme of the text? • Cite evidence for support • Rinse and repeat for other themes • Rewrite TMDLH into ten words • Sustained silent reading	• Bell Ringer • T2 & T3: Comparison activity • Discuss similarities • Discuss differences • Why do these similarities and differences exist? • Sustained silent reading	• CFA 3: AMoCC and AJ • T4: Forced associations, conscious self-deceits, synectics, ethical dilemmas • How is _____ like _____? • Get ideas from [a work we read] to improve [cultural concept]. • I only know about _____. Explain _____ to me. • Suppose you could _____. What would _____? • If _____ never happened, what would be the effect? • How did Puritans create ethical dilemmas?

Source: Adapted from Uinta County School District #1. Used with permission.

Summary

In this chapter, we have presented the eight-step instructional cycle. The first four steps concern planning the cycle and take place *before* teaching the content. Steps 5 through 8 occur over the course of instruction. The entire instructional cycle is focused on students attaining mastery of target content (score 3.0) on a proficiency scale or a small set of related scales. Although this process provides the outline of a plan for instructing students, we now need to turn to the actions teachers take during each class period: the daily lessons that will execute, in detail, the instructional cycle plan just developed. We undertake that discussion in the next chapter.

4

Lesson Planning and Teaching Within the Instructional Cycle

In the previous chapter, we outlined an eight-step process for developing an instructional cycle. We now turn our attention to the details of step 5 in the instructional cycle: planning and teaching daily lessons in the cycle. This step involves aligning specific daily activities with the levels of the proficiency scales. Because proficiency scales describe learning progressions for the priority standards, they are guides for scaffolding the learning you will ask students to undertake. Coupled with the information gained from the preassessment, you can construct a logical progression of daily activities that will align to the progression of the proficiency scale. The planned checks for understanding will provide additional guidance to keep your students and the overall instructional cycle plan on track. As stated in the previous chapter, plan the daily lessons in advance, but view them as flexible and be ready to adjust based on the data from ongoing assessments. In the following sections, we consider in more detail the aspects of daily planning and instruction in a standards-based system, including the following topics.

- Proficiency scales as instructional tools

- Instructional strategies aligned to the levels of the scale

- Lesson types

- Adjustments based on student needs

- Extension and remediation

Proficiency Scales as Instructional Tools

The proficiency scale is the heart of everything that occurs in a standards-based classroom. Sharing proficiency scales with students is essential to any instructional cycle. The proficiency scale clarifies to each student exactly what he or she must know or be able to do to succeed in the instructional cycle. The scale also provides the basis for discussing learning with students. Teachers who begin using proficiency scales with students often report to us that students quickly adopt the language of the scale. In fact, students focus less on the grade they receive in the class and more on the learning with which they are engaged, thus supporting the shift from what is taught to what has been learned. It takes some practice for teachers to continually focus on scales during instruction, but the response of students once they do so makes the shift worthwhile. Having students understand and focus on the proficiency scale is the single most important factor in developing student involvement in their own learning (Moeller et al., 2012).

During the actual teaching of the instructional cycle, the proficiency scale serves as the central touchstone to align everything done in the classroom. The first step is to make proficiency scales readily available as objects of reference in the classroom. There are nearly unlimited ways to do this, but teachers should select methods with which they are comfortable, and which will remind and encourage the teacher to use it often. For many elementary educators, some form of bulletin board or wall display works well. A graphic that is consistent from scale to scale (such as a stairway, balloons gathered in groups of one to four, or an ice-cream cone with multiple scoops; see figure 4.1) can be the basis for this, and the actual content of the scale can change from unit to unit. In the secondary classroom, teachers often provide printed copies of the proficiency scale to their students and ask that students have them readily available in their notebooks. While students will often cooperate with this plan, the way to solve the problem of the student whose notebook is nonexistent or frequently lost is to also have a visual display in the classroom. If you teach from a computer attached to a projector, you can have the scale open as a Word document or a PDF and keep it minimized so you can display it at a moment's notice. Or, just write the scale out on the whiteboard or on a piece of chart paper tacked to the wall.

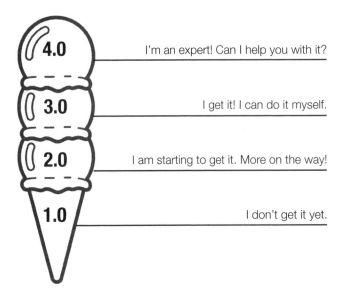

Figure 4.1: Sample scale illustration for elementary classrooms.

During instruction, refer to the scale often—at least once per class session. You will find this challenging at first; it takes instructional time, and you may not think of referencing the scale habitually. With practice it becomes completely natural. In addition to establishing and clarifying the learning target for each lesson, you will find multiple opportunities during class activities or discussions to reference the learning progression of the scale. For example, a student offering an answer to a question creates the opportunity to ask the class questions like the following, which are designed to have students reflect on their understanding of the levels of the scale, and to practice evaluating work as representative of a particular scale level.

- "What level of the scale does that answer reflect?"
- "How do you know? Let's take another look at the scale."

Asking students to apply their understanding of the learning progression and provide explanations based on the proficiency scale both deepens student understanding of the scale itself and reinforces the importance the teacher places on understanding the scale. Our years of experience show that what you, as the teacher, value will eventually emerge in what your students value.

How teachers talk with students about proficiency scales is important, especially when just starting to use scales. Students will likely wonder why a scale is needed at all. Here the teacher can share, briefly, the many ways the class will use scales. But the essential message should be that the scale identifies the learning progression the class is undertaking during a particular instructional cycle. It is often useful to speak in terms of a journey, assembling everything one needs at score 2.0 and gradually making progress toward the goal at score 3.0. Some may want to take the trip a bit further, to score 4.0, but it's not required. This explanation focuses on the learning the class is undertaking and not on a grade. This is another important shift to help students make—away from grades and toward learning. If they undertake the learning progression, the grade will follow.

As teachers start to discuss the specific content they will cover during the journey to score 3.0, exemplars of student work at each level of the scale are an enormous help in building student understanding of performance. Collect exemplars from your classroom, and be sure to obtain permission to use student work. Ideally, these exemplars are anonymous. If it is your first year working with a particular scale, it might be worthwhile to create exemplars yourself as a starting point for building a body of examples. Examples of success at scores 2.0, 3.0, and 4.0 clarify for students the proficiency scale targets that the teacher expects them to achieve. At the secondary level, printing copies of exemplars for students to keep is particularly helpful when dealing with written work. Students can readily understand that their writing will be different at 2.0 than it will at 3.0, and different again at 4.0. The same is true with the depth of analysis in a science lab or the level of understanding in a complex mathematics problem. Having examples of work at each level in their notebooks can be an important reference point when students have their own work scored and returned.

Proficiency scales are also the basis of feedback during the instructional cycle. In providing feedback to students, teachers can use any form they have found effective, but should reference the levels of the scale each time feedback is given. Direct and specific feedback honors the importance of the scale and develops students' understanding of the effects of their hard work and their own status on the learning progression. Feedback has four essential characteristics: it should be timely, specific, clear, and corrective (Marzano, Pickering, & Pollock, 2001). In other words, teachers should provide feedback as soon as possible after the student completes the work, the feedback should refer to specific issues, it should be communicated to the student in terms he or she can understand, and it should give the student the opportunity to correct the errors that he or she has made. The following examples of feedback demonstrate the advantages reference to a proficiency scale can provide.

- **Traditional:** "On the quiz, you got 8 out of 10 correct. That represents an 80 percent, or a grade of B–. Clearly, you still have some work to do on some of the content we've been studying."

- **Scale-based:** "On the most recent assessment, you got most of the questions on the score 2.0 section correct, so good job! The ones you didn't get correct show that we need to work on one specific learning target on score 2.0. You're almost there!"

The first example, representing feedback of the type common with conventional instruction and assessment, provides the student with some understanding of his or her performance but is not specific about what the student knows and is able to do. It provides little instruction about what to do to improve. In the second example, the student understands which specific portions of the content at score 2.0 on the proficiency scale he or she knows, and which ones to focus on to improve. Note also that the teacher can identify success in very specific ways. A proficiency scale with aligned assessments provides a level of specificity that is often impossible with more traditional feedback.

A concern many teachers may have as they move to working with proficiency scales is the effect scales may have on students whose progress is slow or does not keep up with that of the class in general. The scale itself does not create that lack of progress, but as a measurement tool, it makes the lack of progress more obvious, and this can be difficult for a student who is struggling. While we understand this concern, consider that rather than a vehicle for identifying the problem, the proficiency scale can be the vehicle by which the problem can be directly addressed. The scale, coupled with aligned assessments, will show the student the specific areas that require additional work. You can work directly with the student to identify those areas, set incremental goals that will help the student progress, and provide reassurance that he or she can achieve proficiency on the overall standard as well.

The scale helps students see instruction, assessment, and feedback as related to the learning progression. It provides a reference for improvement and helps students understand next steps for that improvement. Coupled with teacher communication centered on the proficiency scale, referencing the proficiency scale deepens students' understanding beyond that provided by comments written in the margins of a paper. And, because the proficiency scale explains the learning progression itself, teachers may find their own marks and comments on student work can be briefer and thus the feedback timelier.

Instructional Strategies Aligned to the Levels of the Scale

As you begin to identify instructional activities for each daily plan, it is essential to align them with the level of the scale that is the focus of a particular daily lesson. The process of aligning learning activities with scale levels can be described in three steps.

1. **Unpack the learning target.** In other words, consider *exactly* what the student must know and be able to do to achieve what is depicted in the learning target.

2. **Determine the cognitive demand of the learning target.** In determining cognitive demand, it is useful to think in terms of the mental processes that a learning target asks students to perform. This usually involves considering two factors: the cognitive demand of the verbs and the cognitive demand of the context. Consider what the verb entails but account for the context and subject of that cognition as well. For example, the verb *describe* often signals a relatively low level of cognitive demand. If we ask a seventh-grade ELA student to describe a metaphor, she may recall a memorized definition, a fairly low level of cognition. If, on the other hand, we ask that same student to describe the development of a character through a novel she has read, the cognitive demand is significantly higher. Context, therefore, matters just as much as the verb.

3. **Select an instructional strategy that matches the learning target's level of cognitive demand.** This involves determining the level of cognitive demand represented by the instructional strategy. Use much the same process as the second step. Consider exactly what an activity asks students to do, keeping in mind the question, What mental processes does this learning target ask students to perform? Teachers will also use their professional expertise in this step. Having experience using a selected instructional strategy is definitely an advantage, but even if the strategy is new, you can analyze the cognitive demand.

As an example, consider how a teacher might align a set of commonly used instructional strategies, such as examining similarities and differences (Marzano Resources, n.d.b), to a level of a proficiency scale. Examining similarities and differences encompasses a wide range of specific instructional strategies. For our example, let's consider a third-grade teacher working on the following ELA standard.

> Describe characters in a story (e.g., their traits, motivations, or feelings) and explain how their actions contribute to the sequence of events. (RL.3.3; NGA & CCSSO, 2010a)

Let us also assume that the class has reached the point in the instructional cycle where they are working toward proficiency on this standard (that is, working at level 3.0 on the proficiency scale). Applying each of the three steps to align instructional strategies to this level 3.0 for this standard, the teacher would do the following.

1. **Unpack the learning target.** Exactly what must third graders do to be proficient in this standard? Identifying characters in a story, their traits, motivations, and feelings would have been skills that were developed earlier in the instructional cycle, at score 2.0. Now, students are asked to put that information into a description and then to explain the connections between the characters' actions and the sequence of events in the story.

This final requirement takes some analysis. Students have to make the connection between the description an author gives of traits and actions and the events in a story. Further, *describe* means more than list traits; it means students must put together that listing of traits into a description, requiring the student to draw some conclusions about the overall qualities of the characters. Those conclusions will be a first step toward drawing the connection between the characters' actions and the events in the story.

2. **Determine the cognitive demand of the learning target.** In this example, students must reason through how the traits they have listed create an overall sense of the qualities of each character, and that will allow them to accurately connect those qualities with adjectives that can create a description. Then, students must apply that thinking toward making the connection with the events of the story. This requires some level of analytical thinking.

3. **Select an instructional strategy that matches the learning target's level of cognitive demand.** In our case, instruction for the learning target at score 3.0 would take several classes and would progress through each of the levels of cognitive demand described in step 2. Early in the class's work on this learning target, students would focus on assembling an accurate description of the characters. Later in the instruction to this learning target, students would use that description and understanding of the characters to analyze the connection to the events of the story.

Early in the score 3.0 instruction, sentence stem comparisons would allow students to examine their growing description of several characters in a story by comparing and contrasting specific traits of those characters. This will allow them to build more accurate descriptions of each character in the story prior to analyzing the characters' connections to events in the story. In choosing sentence stem comparisons and given the context in which the teacher will use the strategy, he or she has aligned that strategy to a specific learning target in the scale. With this in mind, the teacher can ask students to use lists of traits, motivations, and feelings that they will have assembled during instruction for score 2.0 on the scale and have them reason through comparisons that take the following form (Marzano Resources, n.d.b).

- Character A and Character B are similar because they both _____.
- Character A and Character B are different because Character A is _____, but Character B is _____.

Once students have completed this comparison for each of the important characters in the story, they can meet to discuss their findings, refine their understandings, and support their reasoning. This is an important stepping-stone to analyzing the connection of each character to events in the story. Importantly, teachers who conduct this kind of instructional strategy can be assured that their students are being asked to work at the cognitive level required by the learning target.

In high school classrooms, teachers can still use a powerful strategy like examining similarities and differences and the process for aligning activities with levels of the scale. Consider the following level 3.0 learning targets from a history classroom.

- Relate past and present events to one another.

- Critique the effects of past and present events.

- Predict plausible future outcomes based on past events.

Once again, let us follow the three steps for aligning an instructional strategy to the scale level, in this case score 3.0.

1. **Unpack the learning targets.**

   a. *Relate past and present events to one another.* Here students must identify similarities and differences between past and present events.

   b. *Critique the effects of past and present events.* After identifying the effects of each category of events, students must analyze these effects, suggesting whether they are positive or negative in their impacts.

   c. *Predict plausible future outcomes based on past events.* Based on the relationship between past and present events, students must determine the applicability of the patterns they have identified and suggest how those patterns will manifest themselves in future events.

2. **Determine the cognitive demand of the learning targets.**

   a. *Relate past and present events to one another.* The thought process is one of comparison and contrast.

   b. *Critique the effects of past and present events.* The cognitive level of this learning target is more robust than learning target a. Here students must think at the analytical level, making value judgments about the power and impact of the identified events and their effects.

   c. *Predict plausible future outcomes based on past events.* Predicting involves the thought process of induction, where new ideas are based on the perceived patterns of other ideas, in this case events and their effects. Induction is analytical in nature.

3. **Select an instructional strategy that matches the learning targets' level of cognitive demand.** Assuming the teacher intends to address all three learning targets in an instructional strategy, he or she needs one that will lead students to do comparison and contrast and then provide a means for analysis and prediction. Examining similarities and differences is a category of instructional strategies that includes a wide range of cognitive levels. For our purposes here, the teacher might select a comparison matrix—a graphic for representing similarities and differences between things (figure 4.2, page 72)— and modify it slightly so that it includes all three learning targets. Teachers can supply the items and the criteria. Students then record, in the open cells of the matrix, information about the ways in which the criteria are

represented in the items. An analysis of the information thus recorded in the matrix provides a careful and somewhat detailed comparison and contrast of the items. Alternatively, the teacher may provide only the items, or only the criteria, and ask students to provide the rest. In this case, while the results may be less predictable, the depth of thought may be greater.

	Item A	Item B
Criteria A		
Criteria B		

Source: Adapted from Marzano Resources, n.d.b.

Figure 4.2: Blank comparison matrix.

To further illustrate the use of the comparison matrix strategy with these learning targets, consider figure 4.3. Suppose the teacher presents students with the task of creating a timeline of events in World War II, comparing and contrasting them with current events, and then predicting future events. The teacher might then provide students with a comparison matrix with three criteria already identified, and ask students to use the timeline to identify the World War II events that align with the criteria. This would require some discussion, as there will likely be some disagreement about which events best meet the criteria. Once the class has agreed on events, the teacher can then ask students to identify contemporary events that meet the same criteria. Here there will be many different answers, and the class can discuss how appropriate or inappropriate certain events are, given the criteria. At this point, students will be working on learning target a, relating past and present events to one another. In addressing learning target b, critiquing the effects of past and present events, the teacher would ask students to complete the next two columns in the matrix. Here they will think analytically about the information in the columns on World War II events and contemporary events and make judgments about their effects. The teacher can instruct students to be ready to defend their choices with evidence and solid logic. Finally, the teacher asks students to predict analogous future events, using the information in the four columns they have already filled out. This addresses learning target c, predict plausible future outcomes based on past events. Again, the teacher would require students to be able to support their predictions with explanations of how the information on World War II events, contemporary events, and their effects inform their predictions. Discussion among students following this activity will provide serious analysis of the thinking behind the comparison indicated in the matrix. The cognitive demand though, is at the 3.0 level of the scale, based on the learning targets to which the activity aligns.

These examples should make clear that the cognitive demand of instruction is decided by the cognitive demand of the level of the proficiency scale. In other words, the learning target will determine the depth of thought and processing teachers must ask of their students, not some arbitrary notion of what thinking might be at score 2.0 or score 3.0. The degree of cognitive demand will shift from scale to scale, even within a grade level and content area, based on what the learning target requires.

	World War II Event	Contemporary Event	Effects of World War II Events	Effects of Contemporary Events	Future Prediction
Aggressive Starting Events	Germany invades Poland Japan attacks Pearl Harbor	Onset of global pandemic			
Key Turning Point Events	Fall of Stalingrad Battle of Midway	Development and distribution of effective vaccine			
Concluding Events	Invasion of Germany; Germany surrenders Atomic bomb attacks; Japan surrenders	Countries reach herd immunity			

Figure 4.3: Comparison matrix for World War II and contemporary events.

Returning to the seventh-grade ELA instructional cycle that was the subject of planning in the previous chapter, let's briefly take a look at an example of aligning content and strategies. On the proficiency scale for citing textual evidence, the score 2.0 learning targets are "Recognize or recall specific vocabulary, such as *claim, evidence, explicitly, imply, inference*" and "Cite several pieces of evidence that support what an informational text says explicitly." Considering the verbs and the context, the teacher is looking to place students in a situation in which they must use their understanding of the terms *evidence* and *inference* to properly identify examples of each and to eliminate nonexamples of each. In the process of doing so, students refine their understanding of evidence and inference.

The teacher might use an informational text like an excerpt from *Mary Chesnut's Civil War* (Woodward, 1981) as a starting point. Mary Chesnut, born in South Carolina in the 1820s, was married to James Chesnut, a Confederate general in the Civil War. Mary kept a diary throughout the years of the Civil War, and the following excerpt records the day on which, after the war had ended, she received the news of the assassination of President Abraham Lincoln. As with any complex document, the teacher would provide students with a vocabulary list and background information to support a careful reading of the text by a seventh grader.

April 22, 1865. This yellow Confederate quire of paper, my journal, blotted by entries, has been buried three days with the silver sugar-dish, teapot, milk-jug, and a few spoons and forks that follow my fortunes as I wander. With these valuables was Hood's silver cup, which was partly crushed when he was wounded at Chickamauga.

It has been a wild three days. Aides galloping around with messages. Yankees hanging over us like a sword of Damocles. We have been in queer straits. We sat up at Mrs. Bedon's dressed, without once going to bed for forty-eight hours. And we were aweary. Marianna in the grange does not know anything about it. No Yankees spright her or fright her there.

Colonel Cad Jones came with a dispatch, a sealed secret dispatch. It was for General Chesnut. I opened it.

Lincoln—old Abe Lincoln—killed—murdered—Seward wounded!

Why? By whom? It is simply maddening, all this.

I sent off messenger after messenger for General Chesnut. I have not the faintest idea where he is, but I know this foul murder will bring down worse miseries on us.

Mary Darby says: "But they murdered him themselves. No Confederates are in Washington."

"But if they see fit to accuse us of instigating it?"

"Who murdered him?"

"Who knows?"

"See if they don't take vengeance on us, now that we are ruined and cannot repel them any longer."

Met Mr. Heyward. He said: ". . . The death of Lincoln—I call that a warning to tyrants. He will not be the last President put to death in the capital, though he is the first." (Woodward, 1981, p. 791)

To reach the first learning target, the first step is to work with the term *inference*. To develop students' comprehension, teachers might use *concept attainment*, or presenting examples and nonexamples. The teacher presents examples from the passage, and, for each example, students identify whether it is an example or a nonexample of inference and explain their choices. In discussing the examples and nonexamples, students' understanding of inference deepens. Here are a few examples and nonexamples of inferences for the preceding passage.

Examples of inferences:

- Mary hides her diary because she is afraid the Yankees will discover it.

- Mary remained dressed while sitting up all night at Mrs. Bedon's so that she could make a fast escape if necessary.

- Mary feels, as General Chesnut's wife, she has the right to open a dispatch meant for him.

Nonexamples of inferences:

- Mary must live a wartime life that is different than her normal life.

- Citizens of South Carolina must hide their valuables in wartime.

- Mary and her acquaintances are afraid of the consequences of Lincoln's assassination.

The teacher could proceed in much the same way with providing examples and nonexamples of evidence for supporting inferences from the text.

Consider that the cognitive demand of this activity, though substantial, aligns to the score 2.0 level of the scale. Students are building initial knowledge, establishing the foundation of understanding on this topic. This activity prepares students to take their understanding of inference and evidence to the score 3.0 level, so it is a good scaffolding experience for score 2.0. This may take one to two classes. Once that is achieved, students have dealt with an important part of the first learning target in score 2.0: "Recognize or recall specific vocabulary, such as *claim, evidence, explicitly, imply, inference*." Students will likely need some additional practice to hone this skill in another class, but the degree to which this is necessary is left to the teacher to determine. The teacher might use a short assessment to measure their ability at this point, or he or she can simply rely on observational evidence and go on to address the second learning target: "Cite several pieces of evidence that support what an informational text says explicitly." The teacher's best judgment is in play here, but a rule of thumb is, when in doubt, assess. The more specific evidence a teacher has of student abilities, the better his or her decisions will be. As described in the next chapter, an assessment of this kind need not be large or take substantial instructional time. The teacher, at the point of addressing the second learning target, would go through the same alignment process as described above to identify instructional strategies for "Cite several pieces of evidence that support what an informational text says explicitly."

While aligning instructional strategies to the levels of the scale, teachers should also continue to plan for exceptional learners. This includes general instructional supports and IEP supports.

General Instructional Supports

As mentioned previously, general instructional supports can be provided to any student during the opportunity to learn. These supports do not change the grade-level expectations articulated at score 3.0 on the proficiency scale. Some schools and districts elect to create a list of instructional supports that teachers consider when planning instruction. It is challenging to plan instruction that addresses the unique needs of many different students. When a set of general instructional supports is available as a resource to all staff, teachers can draw from the strategies included on the list to plan for instruction that better meets the needs of individual students and small groups of students and thus reaches all learners in a classroom. When a teacher plans and provides such supports, a student may have a higher degree of success in learning the content.

Figure 4.4 (page 76) is a sample list of general instructional supports determined by a thoughtful group of educators who work in varying roles from across the district. Developing a menu of instructional supports as a team is advantageous for ensuring that there are supports on the list for all students, including those with disabilities, English learners, gifted and talented students, and any other student who has a special or unique need. With this in mind, the development team might be comprised of a few classroom teachers, a special education teacher, an English learner teacher, and a reading teacher. In some schools, there are also teachers for gifted and talented students who might contribute to this list.

The intention of a general instructional supports document is for any teacher to draw on the strategies as he or she plans instruction. A teacher or team of teachers can decide whether students need additional instructional support during the class period. For example, suppose a teacher is providing instruction on a score 3.0 learning target: Compare and contrast the themes, settings, and plots of two texts using textual evidence. Since the students are required to compare and contrast in this learning target, providing a graphic organizer may be an appropriate instructional support. Or, another lesson might include a multistep task for students to complete after learning the content. In that case, a task checklist would benefit students.

General Instructional Supports
1.   Access, activate, and make connections to a student's background knowledge.
2.   Provide graphic organizers or mind mapping.
3.   Display reference charts or anchor charts.
4.   Provide a task checklist for completing multistep tasks.
5.   Read directions or text aloud to a student or simplify the language by rephrasing.
6.   Provide video or audio recordings of a lesson, directions, and so on.
7.   Provide visual representations, such as drawings, photographs, and charts.
8.   Use a visual timer.
9.   Provide time and a specific structure for reflection, such as reflection prompts.
10. Provide time for the student to restate content or directions for a task.
11. Provide a sentence starter, sentence frame, or some sort of response organizer.
12. Provide alternate methods for communicating knowledge (for example, verbal, written, drawn, acted out, gestured, using manipulatives).
13. Provide an academic word list.
14. Provide a bilingual dictionary, a glossary, cognates, or translations (when appropriate).
15. Provide native language support (when appropriate).

Source: Adapted from Teton County School District #1. Used with permission.

Figure 4.4: General instructional supports.

Of course, there will be times when a short list of general instructional supports doesn't include something relevant to a particular classroom activity. However, if the list is thoughtfully crafted to include instructional supports that will frequently apply to a range of classroom activities, it can be a helpful tool time and time again during the instructional planning process. And, it does not have to be a static document. In other words, as ideas for additional instructional supports arise during the planning process, you can add them to the list of general instructional supports. Creating a learning environment that is inclusive of all students is an ongoing process.

Individualized Education Program Supports

To effectively plan and instruct for exceptional learners in a standards-based environment, it is critical that teachers know and implement the accommodations or modifications articulated in a student's individualized education program. The order of *know* and *implement* is purposeful: in order to implement the accommodations or modifications, a teacher must first know the specific learning supports he or she must offer to individual students. Information about individual students within a school is communicated in a variety of ways. Therefore, it is paramount that classroom teachers familiarize themselves with how they can gain access to this important information about their students. Once the information is available to a teacher, he or she must become familiar with the supports required for each learner in the classroom.

Once teachers know the allowable and required accommodations or modifications, they can use this information as they plan the daily instruction that makes up an instructional cycle. For example, suppose that day 3 of the instructional cycle is focused on a score 2.0 learning target. As part of the planning process, the teacher or team may decide that providing the accommodation of a quiet work environment will benefit a certain student as he or she reads a text that is part of the opportunity to learn. The student's IEP may or may not delineate this support as an accommodation. Regardless, the teacher may provide it because it does not change the outcome for learning the content. Or, perhaps day 7 of the cycle requires the students to complete a multistep task following some direct instruction. One student's IEP calls for chunking content when multiple steps are required. This accommodation would provide necessary support to the learner as he attempts to complete the multistep task. The end goal of implementing accommodations or modifications is that a student succeeds with the task or acquires the knowledge and skills addressed on the proficiency scale.

In addition to planning for instructional supports and accommodations, there will be occasions when modifications to the learning opportunity are required. A modification increases or decreases the expectations for learning. For example, suppose the instructional cycle includes an activity on day 9 that requires students to provide three pieces of evidence to support a claim. For students requiring modifications that decrease expectations, the teacher may provide options for a student to choose from when supporting a claim. Or for a gifted student, the teacher may require that the student analyzes the evidence that best supports a claim. The reminder here is that the student's IEP should guide any modifications provided for a student.

Lesson Types

In addition to matching the cognitive demand of specific instructional strategies to learning targets, teachers can also think about general types of lessons and which type is most appropriate for each level of the scale. In *The New Art and Science of Teaching*, Marzano (2017) identified three types of lessons.

1. **Direct instruction lessons:** Direct instruction lessons are effective when teachers are offering new information to students, regardless of whether it consists of declarative (factual) or procedural (skills) knowledge. The teacher identifies important information, divides the information into age-appropriate chunks, and uses high-quality processing strategies to help students remember the important information. An example of a typical direct instruction strategy is presenting content in small chunks— delivering information in short, easily handled portions that allow students to process the new content fully before taking on the next chunk. In terms of the instructional cycle, direct instruction lessons occur early in the unit. Teachers will use direct instruction lessons to introduce score 2.0 and score 3.0 content.

2. **Practicing and deepening lessons:** Practicing and deepening lessons move students to a more rigorous understanding of the essential declarative or procedural knowledge. These lessons ask students to work with the content to cultivate understanding and improve fluency. Typical practicing and

deepening strategies include the comparison matrix described earlier in this chapter (page 71). In terms of the instructional cycle, practicing and deepening lessons occur in the middle and latter parts of the unit and apply most often to score 3.0 content.

3. **Knowledge application lessons:** Knowledge application lessons require students to go beyond what was taught in class and thus align well with the 4.0 level of the scale. These lessons include instructional strategies that require students to work independently and apply what they have learned in direct instruction and practicing and deepening lessons. Because they require students to go beyond what is taught in class, teachers should not expect that all students will succeed in these activities. While not every student will succeed in a knowledge application activity, nearly all students will benefit academically by participating in such an activity. That being said, teachers should be careful not to require performance at this level from students who are still struggling with the simpler content of the proficiency scale. An example of a knowledge application instructional strategy is problem solving, where students are presented with a problem that requires them to generate new thinking by applying knowledge they have gained earlier in their learning. In terms of the instructional cycle, knowledge application lessons typically occur near the end of the unit.

In addition to these three types of lessons, there are also strategies that occur in all types of lessons (Marzano, 2017). These strategies can be appropriate no matter what level of instruction the teacher is presenting. Typical of this category are strategies such as previewing, highlighting critical information, and purposeful homework. Obviously, these instructional strategies can occur at any point in the instructional cycle. Figure 4.5 displays how the three types of lessons align with the three levels of content within the proficiency scale.

4.0	In addition to exhibiting level 3 performance, in-depth inferences and applications that go beyond what was taught in class	Knowledge Application Lessons
3.0	No major errors or omissions regarding any of the information or processes (simple or complex) that were explicitly taught	Direct Instruction Lessons *and* Practicing and Deepening Lessons
2.0	No major errors or omissions regarding the simpler details and processes but major errors or omissions regarding the more complex ideas and processes	Direct Instruction Lessons

Source: Adapted from Marzano, 2017.

Figure 4.5: Aligning lesson types to scale levels.

Note that there may be exceptions, such as rare instances where score 2.0 content is the subject of a practicing and deepening lesson, so teachers should not consider this alignment absolute. In teaching the simpler content at level 2.0, teachers will likely use many direct instruction strategies. Most level 2.0 content lends itself to direct instruction strategies for presentation and processing. Note that direct instruction strategies also occur at level 3.0 of the scale. This is because there is new content for teachers to present to students at that level, especially when students are beginning level 3.0. Then, teachers will quickly shift to practicing and deepening lessons that increase the rigor of student understanding and push students to the level of proficiency required at level 3.0. Knowledge application lessons and their associated strategies are often student driven, rely on application of the knowledge from level 3.0, and are ideal for level 4.0 of the scale.

Although a deep discussion of the over three hundred strategies included in Marzano's (2017, 2019) *The New Art and Science of Teaching* model is beyond the scope of our analysis, a review of sample strategies in each category, as shown in table 4.1 (page 80), will give you a better understanding of what typically occurs during instruction at each level of the proficiency scale. *The New Art and Science of Teaching* model's delineation of instructional strategies by lesson type in this manner provides a convenient menu of options for teachers designing lessons by proficiency scale level.

Adjustments Based on Student Needs

The instructional cycle plan, along with individual lesson plans, provides the overview of what will happen day by day, but teachers will make adjustments to the plan based on what formative assessment data tell them about how students are learning. If a teacher finds that the instructional cycle plan calls for moving to practicing and deepening strategies for level 3.0 content, but formative assessment data suggest students are not yet competent with the level 2.0 content, that teacher would adjust the plan to do some reteaching. In doing so, the teacher selects a direct instruction strategy that allows students to process the score 2.0 content, such as combination notes (using words and drawings) or a graphic organizer. Likewise, if students are well into the unit and the instructional cycle plan assumes they are proficient with score 3.0 content, formative assessment data might suggest that students need additional practicing and deepening lessons to reach mastery. Once again, a list of strategies for this lesson type will provide teachers with many suggestions about how to offer students additional opportunities to move their understanding to a more rigorous level. Students might engage in practicing and deepening strategies such as sentence stem comparison (see page 70) or a comparison matrix (see page 71) to provide additional practice on essential score 3.0 content before attempting to apply their knowledge with a score 4.0 knowledge application activity.

To make these adjustments in real time, teachers must consider background knowledge, context, cognitive demand, and where students are in their learning. Once again, the great advantage of the proficiency scale is that it provides teachers with a framework to align strategies to the learning progression on the standard.

Extension and Remediation

Toward the end of an instructional cycle, you will need to differentiate lessons to accommodate students who are proficient and need additional challenge as well as students who need more help to master the content.

Table 4.1: Lesson Types and Example Strategies

Category	Subcategory	Sample Strategy
Direct Instruction Lessons	Chunking Content	Presenting content in small chunks: The teacher divides the content into small "digestible" portions for students.
	Processing Content	Collaborative processing: The teacher places students into small groups to summarize information, ask questions to clarify the content, and make predictions about upcoming content.
	Recording and Representing Content	Graphic organizers: Students record their learning in an organizer that corresponds to patterns found in information.
Practicing and Deepening Lessons	Using Structured Practice Sessions	Guided practice: The teacher provides structured opportunities, moving from simple to more complex, for students to learn new skills, strategies, or processes.
	Examining Similarities and Differences	Venn diagrams: The teacher provides a visual tool to compare and contrast two or three people, events, concepts, or processes.
	Examining Errors in Reasoning	Finding errors in the media: The teacher provides students with examples of media reporting of news events, commercials, blogs, and other sources and asks them to find and analyze errors in reasoning that underlie the messages therein.
Knowledge Application Lessons	Engaging Students in Cognitively Complex Tasks	Problem-solving tasks: The teacher uses problem-solving tasks to teach students how to set a goal, identify obstacles to reaching that goal, find solutions, predict which solution is most likely to work, test their prediction, examine the results, evaluate the results, and reflect on the process.
	Providing Resources and Guidance	Interviews: The teacher conducts interviews with students to keep track of their progress as they work on cognitively complex projects and tasks.
	Generating and Defending Claims	Presenting the formal structure of claims and support: The teacher provides students with formal distinctions for the elements of claims and support, including grounds, backing, and qualifiers.

Source: Adapted from Marzano, 2017, 2019.

To extend the learning for students who have mastered the score 3.0 content, provide activities at level 4.0 of the proficiency scale. As we will show in the subsequent example (page 82), these activities can be a central part of the plan for the instructional cycle, even though not every student participates in them. By providing knowledge application activities, students who are proficient at score 3.0 content extend their abilities, and students who are partially proficient at score 3.0 content continue to build toward mastery. For this reason, it may be beneficial to offer knowledge application activities to students who are demonstrating partial proficiency, at score 2.5, for example. Again, the classroom teacher will be the best judge of what is best for his or her students in this regard.

One of the unique qualities of knowledge application activities is that they are student driven. In other words, students act independently once the activity has been organized, and the teacher moves into the facilitator role. This generally frees teacher instructional time to focus on students in need of remediation. In this way, the instructional cycle plan offers the possibility of differentiation in the classroom, without substantial logistical changes such as reorganizing the physical space or providing different textbooks or other resources to different groups of students.

Students who are having more difficulty mastering the score 2.0 and score 3.0 content will need remediation. In making these adjustments in response to student needs, you may find that a significant portion of students are not on track to master the standards by the end of the unit. This requires you to decide whether to extend the instructional cycle or move on to the next one. This is not an easy decision, but it represents the real world for most teachers. We suggest that you consider three factors in making the decision of whether to move on to the next instructional cycle.

1. **The complexity of the priority standards in the current instructional cycle:** Is this the ideal moment to pursue deeper understanding or would an instructional cycle later in the year align better with the students' cognitive development? Here the consideration is the current status of the students' development. Some students need additional intellectual maturation before they can readily reach proficiency on more complex academic topics that they may encounter later in the year.

2. **The time of the year in which the current instructional cycle is being taught:** Will the current standard come up again later in the year with different or more complex content or is this the only opportunity for students to obtain the learning? In other words, if the teacher decides to move on without mastery early in the year, he or she must ensure that there is another opportunity to reach mastery on that standard later in the year. This differs from the previous factor in that it focuses on the role of the standard rather than the intellectual readiness of the student.

3. **Time allowances in the current instructional cycle for interventions and extensions:** Does the current instructional cycle offer additional time or not? This decision concerns the viability of the overall curriculum. If the teacher spends more time on simpler content and standards early in the year, will there be time for more complex priority standards later in the year? This is often the most challenging factor, and the choice is a complex one. Is it worth spending the time now, getting simpler content and skills solidly in place, so that students can master more complex skills in less instructional time?

As you can see, the question of whether to move on to the next instructional cycle is complex, and we cannot offer one formula that fits every situation. By considering these issues, however, teachers are more likely to arrive at a decision that is in the best interests of the class. While foundational knowledge is important for all students, adding additional time to solidify this foundation for some students creates the problem of delaying further educational development of other students. Many students in the class will benefit from an additional challenge when they are ready rather than waiting for their peers to catch up. Providing differentiated instruction (opportunities for both extension and intervention as needed) at the end of the unit is a solution, but there is also a point of diminishing returns for your most advanced students.

A Sample Lesson-Planning Process

To see how the process of planning and delivering lessons works within an instructional cycle plan, let's refer to the example unit from the previous chapter. In this case, the priority standard is on citing textual evidence. As a reminder, figure 4.6 displays the proficiency scale for this standard. Figure 4.7 displays the full instructional cycle plan for the seventh-grade ELA unit on citing textual evidence.

Grade 7 ELA
Citing Textual Evidence

7.RI.KID.1 — Cite several pieces of textual evidence to support analysis of what the text says explicitly as well as inferences drawn from the text.	
Score 4.0	In addition to score 3.0, the student demonstrates in-depth inferences or application of knowledge. For example, the student will: • Analyze the quality of textual evidence used to support an inference
Score 3.0	The student will: • Cite several pieces of textual evidence that support an inference in informational text
Score 2.0	The student will: • Recognize or recall specific vocabulary, such as *claim*, *evidence*, *explicitly*, *imply*, *inference* • Cite several pieces of evidence that support what an informational text says explicitly
Score 1.0	With help, the student demonstrates knowledge of some score 2.0 and score 3.0 content.

Source for standard: Archdiocese of Chicago, n.d.b.

Figure 4.6: Proficiency scale for citing textual evidence.

As the teacher begins to develop daily lesson plans for the start of this cycle, note that she is unlikely to have data from the day 1 preassessment to inform the daily lesson plan for day 1. That is just fine because there are regular, preliminary tasks for the start of every instructional cycle, such as sharing the proficiency scale with students, explaining the learning progression, and providing students with exemplars of work at each level of the scale. If the teacher has time or needs to move to content instruction on day 1, she can start with vocabulary instruction on the key terms found at level 2.0 of the scale. This is information that all students will need, whether it is new to them or a refresher.

After examining the data from the preassessment, the teacher can adjust any plan she has by modifying or repositioning teaching strategies in the instructional cycle plan so that the sequence best meets her students' needs as indicated by the data. In general, the teacher would plan through the first few days assuming most students would start at the beginning of the learning progression with level 2.0 content. If some students need remedial teaching, she can adjust to that and then begin the move up the scale. While the instructional cycle plan is designed carefully to move students along the learning progression, it will be ineffective if it is not flexible and adjustable to the needs of students.

Instructional Cycle 1: Citing Textual Evidence 14 to 16 days Standards: **7.RI.KID.1**, 7.RL.CAS.6, 7.RI.CAS.4			
SMART goal: By the end of the cycle for citing textual evidence, 75 percent of students will demonstrate mastery of the priority standard, with all students demonstrating growth.			
Day 1	**Day 2**	**Day 3**	**Day 4**
Citing Textual Evidence Preassessment Daily Lesson Plan 1	Daily Lesson Plan 2	Daily Lesson Plan 3	Check for Understanding 1 Daily Lesson Plan 4
Day 5	**Day 6**	**Day 7**	**Day 8**
Daily Lesson Plan 5	Daily Lesson Plan 6	Check for Understanding 2 Daily Lesson Plan 7	Daily Lesson Plan 8
Day 9	**Day 10**	**Day 11**	**Day 12**
Daily Lesson Plan 9	Check for Understanding 3 Daily Lesson Plan 10	Daily Lesson Plan 11	Daily Lesson Plan 12
Day 13	**Day 14**	**Day 15**	**Day 16**
Citing Textual Evidence End-of-Cycle Assessment	Daily Lesson Plan 14 Writing Activity	Daily Lesson Plan 15 Reteaching, Reinforcement, Enrichment	Daily Lesson Plan 16 Reteaching, Reinforcement, Enrichment

Source for standards: Archdiocese of Chicago, n.d.b.

Figure 4.7: Sample instructional cycle plan, grade 7 ELA.

The instructional cycle plan indicates a check for understanding on day 4, so the first consideration is what content the teacher will address by that day. Again, this will likely consist of vocabulary terms and prerequisite or background knowledge. The level 2.0 learning targets for this unit are as follows.

- Recognize or recall specific vocabulary, such as *claim, evidence, explicitly, imply, inference.*

- Cite several pieces of evidence that support what an informational text says explicitly.

The vocabulary terms such as *inference, evidence,* and *explicitly* are key to the background knowledge and skills. So, on day 1, day 2, or both, the teacher would present this vocabulary instruction. She could use several direct instruction strategies to introduce and reinforce the vocabulary terms. For example, she might use a strategy like chunking content to introduce the terms in digestible bites that students can manage (Marzano, 2019). Once students have a firm understanding of the meaning of each term and know that the next step will be to identify examples of each of these terms in a text, the teacher might provide a processing activity like concept attainment (Marzano, 2019). In this activity, the teacher provides examples and nonexamples of each concept and asks students to identify, compare, and contrast them. Such an activity would prepare students to independently identify inferences in a text.

On day 3, the teacher turns her attention to the second score 2.0 learning target, "Cite several pieces of evidence that support what an informational text says explicitly." Considering the context of the verb in this learning target, an important embedded skill is whether the student can explain the explicit meaning of a text. Clearly, being able to explain what a text explicitly says is a stepping-stone to identifying evidence and, more important, identifying inferences in the text, which will be vital to success at score 3.0. Inference is a level of comprehension beyond explicit meaning, so instruction that explains explicit meaning must come first. Considering that explaining what a text says explicitly is a piece of the learning target at score 2.0, the teacher must then examine the verb, *explain*, and the context of that verb. The teacher would want to select an activity that leads the student to the right level of cognitive demand. This might mean taking an informational text of several paragraphs one paragraph at a time, identifying the topic sentence and major points, and then drawing a conclusion about the explicit meaning of that paragraph. Later, the teacher might ask students to look at the overall result of that process across the paragraphs and draw conclusions about the overall explicit meaning of the text. Depending on students' background knowledge, this instruction may take multiple classes, so the teacher might determine that the assessment on day 4 will only address vocabulary and explaining explicit meaning. She would then plan instruction on the remaining elements of the score 2.0 learning targets (citing textual evidence for explicit meaning) for days 5, 6, and beyond. For the purpose of our example, let's assume the class can accomplish explaining explicit meaning on day 3.

By day 4, the teacher might be ready to provide a text to students and guide them to independently identify evidence and inference, as required by the score 2.0 learning target. While independence is the goal, at this stage, students are likely unsure of their own judgment, so the teacher might choose a processing strategy like think-pair-share to allow students to initially identify examples of each concept on their own, then pair with a partner to confirm their ideas, and eventually share their findings with the entire class.

The class is now ready for the check for understanding on day 4. The teacher has many options for the format of this check. She might simply have students review the proficiency scale and self-assess where they feel they are on the scale. Or, she could give a short paper-and-pencil quiz with questions about each learning target. Analyzing response patterns on the quiz will quickly reveal where the students are on the learning progression. Are they ready for the additional score 2.0 learning targets? Are they ready for score 3.0 content? Does their performance suggest they need additional practice with score 2.0 content? With this information, the teacher can adjust the instructional cycle plan to meet the students where they are.

Before we proceed, though, we should never ignore the possibility of celebrating success! This check for understanding will show progress. We shouldn't assume students are aware of how much they have already learned: they need recognition, whether they are primary students, high school seniors, or anyone in between. Students have learned over many years of traditional teaching and assessment to focus on what they did wrong. It's time to help them see what they are doing right! There are many ways to accomplish these celebrations, and they can be fairly simple actions that have a strong effect. Depending on the grade level and the particular classroom culture, simply ringing a bell or leading the class in group applause could be used to signify that some students have made knowledge gains or improved their status on the proficiency scale (Marzano, 2017). Celebrations of progress also provide an ideal time to revisit the proficiency scale as a learning progression and reinforce its importance in students' understanding of their own progress.

It is likely that the students will need some additional practice at score 2.0 content, but let's assume that this requires only a single day's instruction. The teacher can use the same instructional strategies but increase the challenge of the sample text. If students make good progress, they can begin to work on the additional score 2.0 learning targets, citing evidence for explicit meaning. If not, the teacher can easily adjust the instructional cycle plan to support that need.

One common question teachers have about any plan for instruction is, When is it time to move on? In other words, How do I know when enough of my students are ready for higher-level content? In a traditional teaching situation, where content drives the curriculum, this question rarely appears because the class moves on when the pacing of the content dictates, regardless of student learning levels. Teachers often do not have formative assessment data but rely on the textbook as the curriculum plan and just keep going. For many students, this means falling further and further behind as the unit progresses. In the case of standards-based planning and instruction, the proficiency scale and aligned assessments provide the formative data to inform decisions about when to proceed to more challenging content. There is no hard-and-fast rule about moving up the scale. The teacher's best judgment is really the answer, but that judgment is informed by a real understanding of the *learning* that has taken place rather than the teaching. It is grounded in the learning progression of the proficiency scale and aligned assessments that provide the data showing student progress on that scale. It's not enough that you've taught it; have your students learned it? If the majority of the class is ready to move up the scale, then it is likely a good move to proceed. If the majority has not, clearly more work is needed on the lower levels of content. But the decision is rarely that clear. In the end, the teacher must choose what is best for most students, but then must *also* meet the needs of the rest of the class. That means differentiation as we discussed earlier in this chapter (page 79), but the great advantage of working with a proficiency scale is that you will know the specific needs of the students that need remediation. There are also the larger considerations about time devoted to the instructional cycle, and how extending the instructional cycle impacts other instructional cycles, as discussed on page 81.

For the purposes of our example, let us assume that students are ready to begin work on score 3.0 content on day 6. Here is the 3.0 learning target from the proficiency scale: "Cite several pieces of textual evidence that support an inference in informational text." Obviously this skill builds well off the content taught at score 2.0, which involved understanding and identifying inferences and what a text says explicitly. It will be important for the teacher to point out that progression to students to assure them that what they already know and can do will help them achieve proficiency on these new skills.

The first consideration is that the instructional cycle plan suggests a second check for understanding on day 7. The teacher can use this opportunity to get students' first reaction to score 3.0 content through a simple check-in about their understanding of their own progress on the proficiency scale rather than a formal quiz. This brief check might involve students indicating where they believe they are on the proficiency scale by raising a number of fingers or filling in a number on a piece of paper. Because the class will subsequently have more time to learn score 3.0 content, the teacher can plan to give a more thorough check for understanding on day 10.

As noted previously, teaching score 3.0 begins with direct instruction lessons. The 3.0 learning target requires the teacher to present and model the process. Students will need to understand how to select evidence that supports an inference and to cite that evidence. But the teacher can now rely on students' solid understanding of explicit meaning and inferences as she instructs them in these skills.

To begin teaching the score 3.0 learning target, the teacher would chunk the steps of citing textual evidence for the inferential meaning of a text into individual pieces and provide examples for each step. These steps might include identifying possible evidence in the text, recording that evidence in some manner, organizing the potential evidence into categories, and using a step-by-step process for judging which evidence best supports claims about the inferential meaning of the text. Finally, students would receive instruction about how to cite the evidence they have selected. The teacher would likely use direct instruction strategies to help students understand and process these chunks. The class would then proceed to the practicing and deepening strategy of modeling. Here the teacher works through a text, identifying inferential meaning and specific evidence for that meaning. The teacher would explain, in some detail, the reasoning supporting the choices she is making. Students would then ask any clarifying questions they have. Then the teacher and students would go through the process together with another text, with the students participating instead of observing. If they succeed on this example, students could analyze a third text, this time independently. As with score 2.0 instruction, the teacher can support students' growing appreciation of their own analysis by having them pair with each other and share. They will often find they are making the same decisions as their partners, and their confidence in their own ability to follow the steps of the process will grow.

Well into teaching score 3.0 content, the teacher may want to plan a check-in with the SMART goal for the unit. The goal for this sample instructional cycle is for 75 percent of students to demonstrate mastery of the priority standard and for all students to demonstrate growth. Once the class has moved into score 3.0 content, the teacher will want to keep the goal in mind. The assessment data should begin to give her an idea of whether the class will reach it. As always, as the instructional cycle proceeds, the teacher can adjust daily lesson plans to align with achieving the SMART goal. For example, as the instructional cycle progresses and the teacher monitors data from the formative assessments given in the cycle, the data may indicate that 60 to 75 percent of students are demonstrating growth and are near to score 3.0 proficiency. These data indicate that the SMART goal is in reach, but the class is not quite there. Additional work on score 3.0 is likely needed to get them over the finish line. The teacher would then adjust the instructional cycle plan, and in the case of this example, it might simply mean an additional practicing and deepening activity to move the class toward proficiency.

As the daily lessons of the instructional cycle plan proceed, the class will continue to practice the skill of establishing inferential meaning and supporting claims about that meaning with evidence using increasingly challenging texts. In this example, opportunities for independent practice present themselves on days 7, 8, 9, 10, 11, and 12. Should teachers give students independent practice on all of those days? It depends on the progress students are making. If they establish the ability to perform, in this case, at level 3.0 in each skill on the first day of independent practice, there seems little reason to continue to provide those opportunities. Some students may need that practice and others may not. Students who do not need that additional practice might begin work on a knowledge application activity.

Ideally, most of the students will be adept with citing textual evidence to support inferences by day 13 of the instructional cycle, and they will be ready for a formal end-of-cycle assessment that asks students to apply the skills they have been practicing with a text they have not seen before. Formative data from that assessment will provide the evidence the teacher needs to decide whether some students can move beyond score 3.0 on days 15 and 16.

On day 14, the instructional cycle plan gives students an opportunity to apply the score 3.0 skills in a written assignment. This in-class writing assignment also provides the teacher time to score the end-of-cycle assessment given the previous day. In the ELA classroom, such a writing activity is very important because it applies the process of citing textual evidence for inferential meaning at the score 3.0 level. This writing activity would differ from the end-of-cycle assessment in that it requires a comprehensive written piece, while the end-of-cycle assessment likely does not. Because students need to cite evidence for inferences on informational text, an end-of-cycle assessment might ask them to provide short, non-narrative answers in a number of scenarios. An assessment of this type requires teachers to spend some time scoring it, but it may not require students to apply their skill in citing evidence in a full written piece. In creating a piece of writing, students are taking the skill of citing evidence and using it in context.

The last few days of an instructional cycle are when adjustment to student needs is most important. It's not always an ideal situation. Although there is a clear SMART goal that establishes, in this case, that 75 percent of students need to be proficient by the end of the instructional cycle, the reality is that the end-of-cycle assessment may show the class falling somewhat short of that goal. The teacher must consider whether the class can reach the goal through two additional days of remediation. If so, there's a clear direction of what to do on those two days. If, however, the teacher determines her class cannot reach the goal, she must grapple with the decision of whether to add days to the current instructional cycle or move on to the next one.

So, what does this moment in the instructional cycle look like in the classroom? For the purposes of this example, let's assume that 60 percent of the class has consistently achieved at score 3.0 by the assessment on day 13 of the instructional cycle. Most of the other 40 percent are performing at a score of 2.5. Perhaps there are one or two students who have yet to fully achieve score 2.0 performance consistently. What should the teacher do for days 15 and 16 in the instructional cycle? Clearly, this situation requires differentiation.

Imposing as that may sound, in a standards-based system with clearly defined levels of instructional strategies and clear data on the performance of the entire class, teachers are well positioned to offer that differentiation. Over half the class can benefit from either additional score 3.0 practice or the challenge of score 4.0 activities. However, a large portion of the class needs additional instruction and practice to reach score 3.0, with a couple of students needing true interventions to help them grow toward proficiency.

For the 40 percent of the class who remain below proficiency, the teacher might start with some additional direct instruction, perhaps engaging instructional strategies in that category that she did not use previously. Students might work in groups using collaborative processing (page 80) or reciprocal teaching (Marzano, 2019) where a group leader questions members of the group on the content presented and members of the group discuss the content. Following the discussion, someone from the group summarizes the content. Strategies such as this allow students to revisit and refine their existing knowledge and prepare for practicing and deepening activities that will then be more effective in moving students along the learning progression of the proficiency scale.

For students who are ready for extension, the teacher can offer score 4.0 activities on days 15 and 16. By definition, score 4.0 activities represent cognitive demand that is beyond what is taught in class. Not every student will reach score 4.0; indeed, it may be the case that most are unable to perform at that level. The goal (and expectation) is to get every student to score 3.0 performance, but score 4.0 is there for those who are able and interested.

Score 4.0 is often where knowledge application lessons come in. Decision making, investigation, experimental inquiry, and the like genuinely challenge students to apply their understanding of the 3.0 content in novel ways. As such, the teacher might choose to offer students an activity that demonstrates in-depth inferences and applications of knowledge, such as the example listed on the proficiency scale: Analyze the quality of textual evidence used to support an inference.

For the daily lesson plans on days 15 and 16, the teacher might offer an activity in which students identify criteria for making judgments about the quality of evidence for inferential meaning, then apply that judgment to compare and contrast specific examples. Consider the teacher's role in this activity: she organizes it, answers students' questions beforehand, and can be available for guidance as students need it; however, students engage in the activity independently. This provides the opportunity for the teacher to work with students who need additional teaching at score 3.0 and score 2.0.

Figure 4.8 displays the complete instructional cycle plan with specific activities for each lesson plan. It is likely the teacher designed most of these daily lesson plans before giving the preassessment on day 1. Indeed, year by year, teachers will gain a better understanding generally of how their students will proceed through the instructional cycle. This daily plan is designed to be flexible and to change at any moment in response to specific students' needs—not only those needs identified through formative assessment but also those based on what the teacher observes on a daily basis. No daily lesson plans for the instructional cycle should ever be considered written in stone; student learning determines the next step at any moment in the cycle.

Instructional Cycle 1: Citing Textual Evidence 14 to 16 days Standards: **7.RI.KID.1**, 7.RL.CAS.6, 7.RI.CAS.4			
SMART goal: By the end of the cycle for citing textual evidence, 75 percent of students will demonstrate mastery of the priority standard, with all students demonstrating growth.			
Day 1	**Day 2**	**Day 3**	**Day 4**
Citing Textual Evidence Preassessment Daily Lesson Plan 1: Vocabulary instruction	Daily Lesson Plan 2: Vocabulary instruction and concept attainment for evidence and inference Student goal setting for the cycle	Daily Lesson Plan 3: Process for determining explicit textual meaning	Check for Understanding 1 Daily Lesson Plan 4: Instruction for citing evidence on explicit meaning
Day 5	**Day 6**	**Day 7**	**Day 8**
Daily Lesson Plan 5: Additional practice for evidence of explicit textual meaning and supporting evidence	Daily Lesson Plan 6: Direct instruction and modeling of process steps for citing several pieces of evidence for inferential meaning (start score 3.0)	Check for Understanding 2 Daily Lesson Plan 7: Additional refinement and practice of skills of citing several pieces of evidence for inferential meaning	Daily Lesson Plan 8: Additional refinement and practice of skills of citing several pieces of evidence for inferential meaning
Day 9	**Day 10**	**Day 11**	**Day 12**
Daily Lesson Plan 9: Additional refinement and practice of skills of citing several pieces of evidence for inferential meaning	Check for Understanding 3 Daily Lesson Plan 10: Additional refinement and practice of skills of citing several pieces of evidence for inferential meaning	Daily Lesson Plan 11: Additional refinement and practice of skills of citing several pieces of evidence for inferential meaning with new grade-level texts	Daily Lesson Plan 12: Additional refinement and practice of skills of citing several pieces of evidence for inferential meaning with new grade-level texts
Day 13	**Day 14**	**Day 15**	**Day 16**
Citing Textual Evidence End-of-Cycle Assessment	Daily Lesson Plan 14: Applying the skill at score 3.0 in a writing activity	Daily Lesson Plan 15: Reteaching, Reinforcement, Enrichment—Some students work at developing and applying criteria for quality of evidence; others engage in remedial instruction	Daily Lesson Plan 16: Reteaching, Reinforcement, Enrichment—Some students work at developing and applying criteria for quality of evidence; others engage in remedial instruction

Source for standards: Archdiocese of Chicago, n.d.b.

Figure 4.8: Sample instructional cycle plan with daily lesson plans.

Summary

This chapter examined the process of planning and teaching lessons. Using a proficiency scale as the basis for instruction clarifies what to teach and how to adjust for student learning. Aligning instructional strategies and lesson types to the intended level of the proficiency scale for any particular daily lesson in the instructional cycle improves teaching and learning. Once you master this approach, it will also help you adjust the instructional cycle plan to the needs of your students as indicated by formative assessment data. In the next chapter, we will examine topics related to measuring and tracking student progress during the instructional cycle.

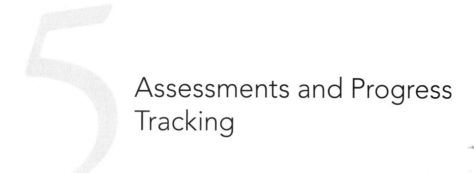

5 Assessments and Progress Tracking

The introduction to *A Teacher's Guide to Standards-Based Learning* (Heflebower et al., 2019) stated:

> When standards-based learning is happening in the classroom, the content taught won't change very much. Even the teaching strategies that teachers use won't change much. But how teachers think about *what* and *how* they teach will change profoundly. (p. 3)

The truth of this statement will likely be apparent after reviewing our discussion of planning and teaching in a standards-based classroom up to this point. The one area of teaching in which traditional forms do not serve students or teachers well in a standards-based classroom, and in which teachers will experience the largest degree of change, is that of assessment.

Assessment is an essential part of the standards-based classroom. Of course, assessment for standards-based learning is different in format and purpose from traditional assessments. Rather than testing at the end of a unit to assign a percentage or letter grade, assessment occurs throughout the instructional cycle to inform teaching and learning, and the data from these assessments are used formatively to make instructional decisions. The levels of knowledge and skill that students demonstrate on an assessment show the teacher where to go next. In terms of the instructional cycle, assessments are most prominent in step 3 (planning to collect evidence of student learning), step 6 (administering and scoring end-of-cycle assessments), and step 7 (implementing the assessment data protocol). In this chapter, we discuss several topics to ensure you can use assessments effectively to enhance student learning.

- Assessments aligned to proficiency scales
- Scores based on proficiency scales
- Student goal setting and tracking

Although we provide this basic information to help readers understand the role and design of assessments to inform their standards-based planning and teaching practices, a detailed discussion of assessment is beyond the scope of this work. For additional information specific to standards-based assessments, readers should consult *The Teacher as Assessment*

Leader (Guskey, 2009), *Formative Assessment and Standards-Based Grading* (Marzano, 2010), *Collaborative Teams That Transform Schools* (Marzano et al., 2016), *Making Classroom Assessments Reliable and Valid* (Marzano, 2018), and *A Teacher's Guide to Standards-Based Learning* (Heflebower et al., 2019).

Assessments Aligned to Proficiency Scales

Just as instructional strategies must be aligned with levels of the learning progression, assessment items must be aligned with the levels of the proficiency scale if they are to report student progress along that learning progression. A student who must recall the meaning of a vocabulary term at score 2.0 would perform a very different assessment task than a student who must compare two complex concepts at level 3.0. Thus, the assessment task must match the scale level which it assesses. Aligned assessments provide an excellent method for giving students specific, useful feedback on their progress along the learning progression described by the proficiency scale. As Marzano (2010) stated, "With a well-articulated sequence of knowledge and skills . . . it is much easier to provide students with feedback as to their current status regarding a specific learning goal and what they must do to progress" (p. 11). Proficiency scales and aligned assessments allow teachers to provide specificity in feedback, identifying for students the specific areas of success on an assessment as well as a specific focus for improvement.

The importance of alignment becomes apparent when one considers how data from these assessments are used. Assessment data provide information that can be used formatively to make decisions about instruction during the unit. Teachers need to know whether students are learning what has been taught *as instruction proceeds through the unit.* Assessments that report data by scale level make it easy to decide if changes need to be made to the overall unit plan. Teachers can readily see from the assessment results if their students need additional lessons at score 2.0, for example, before they take on instruction at score 3.0. With aligned assessment information in hand, teachers can make informed decisions.

The format of an aligned assessment may be somewhat different than traditional assessments. Some mid-unit assessments or checks for understanding will cover only one level of the scale, while others will cover all three levels. An assessment with a narrow focus, measuring, for example, student performance on the score 2.0 vocabulary learning targets, would include questions only on that content, and thus assess only one portion of one level of the scale. Assessments designed to assess most or all of the content on the proficiency scale will include assessment items designed to measure students' performance at scores 2.0, 3.0, and 4.0. Each of these assessments has a place in the instructional cycle, depending on the purpose for which each assessment is designed.

On assessments that cover all three levels, since assessment items are aligned to the proficiency scale, it makes sense to group the items by scale level. Thus, students encounter a section of the assessment that contains only score 2.0 items, then another section of score 3.0 items, and a third section of score 4.0 items. As explained previously, the lower levels of the scale (scores 1.0 and 0.0) do not contain specific content and thus do not require dedicated assessment items. A student's performance on the score 2.0 and score 3.0 items will indicate if a score below 2.0 is appropriate. For example, a student who can achieve partial success on score 2.0 or score 3.0 items but only with teacher assistance would receive a score of 1.0.

While assessment items are grouped together by proficiency scale level, there will likely be a different number of assessment items for each level. The majority of assessment items would likely fall at score 3.0. It is here that teachers need sufficient evidence of proficiency, and most standards require many different aspects of the standard to be assessed, leading to more items. The next largest number of items would come at score 2.0. While we do recommend this as a general rule, many teachers find that the nature of score 2.0 content lends itself to large numbers of score 2.0 questions, and they may number more than the score 3.0 items. The proficiency scale, its aligned content, and the detail with which a teacher must assess items at score 2.0 and score 3.0 may demand some flexibility on this issue. At score 4.0, only one or two items may be necessary because each one is more complex and requires a longer response.

In aligning assessment items to levels of the proficiency scale, teachers use a process similar to aligning instructional activities to levels of the scale (see page 68). Adjusting that process to aligning assessment items, we can identify the steps as follows.

1. Identify the learning targets to be assessed.

2. Determine the cognitive demand of the learning targets to be assessed.

3. Create assessment items that match the learning targets' cognitive demand.

In determining the learning targets to be assessed, teachers must start with a clear understanding of the purpose of a particular assessment. This includes consideration of where the assessment falls in the instructional cycle. An assessment early in the instructional cycle might reasonably include only the learning targets that have been addressed. An assessment in the middle of the instructional cycle might include assessment items for all learning targets in the scale if they have been included in instruction. Late in the instructional cycle, teachers will likely assess the entire scale and all its learning targets. If the purpose of the assessment is only to gather formative data for instructional decisions, this may mean a narrow focus to the assessment. If the purpose of the assessment moves beyond formative data to providing students with detailed information about their progress on multiple learning targets, the scope of the assessment expands. Teachers will need to keep these factors in mind in deciding which learning targets to assess.

As with aligning instructional strategies, the tasks the assessment presents to students will differ with the cognitive demand at each level of the scale. Refer to the previous chapter for a discussion of the second step of this process (page 69), determining cognitive demand.

In the third step of this process, creating an assessment item that matches the cognitive demand of the learning target, we must consider that assessment items at each level of the scale will differ. Teachers should also remember the role of resources at this point; curriculum content is represented by the proficiency scale rather than sections of a resource like a textbook. What teachers assess is student progress in the knowledge and skill identified in the proficiency scale, not the degree to which students understand a resource. With that in mind, you can craft aligned assessment items at each level of the scale.

An example may clarify how assessment items change at different levels of the proficiency scale. Once again, we will refer to the grade 7 ELA proficiency scale for citing textual evidence (see figure 4.6, page 82, for the complete scale). For the purposes of the example, assume that the teacher wants to include learning targets at scores 2.0, 3.0, and 4.0 in the assessment. To organize which learning targets, which scale levels, how many questions, and what type of questions will be on the assessment, the teacher uses a chart called an *assessment blueprint*, shown in figure 5.1.

Assessment Blueprint

Content Area: ELA **Grade Level:** 7

Instructional Cycle: Citing textual evidence

Priority Standard: 7.RI.KID.1

Learning Targets	Score 2.0 Number of questions / Type	Score 3.0 Number of questions / Type	Score 4.0 Number of questions / Type
Recognize or recall specific vocabulary, such as *claim*, *evidence*, *explicitly*, *imply*, *inference*.	5 / Matching		
Cite several pieces of evidence that support what an informational text says explicitly.	4 / Short answer		
Cite several pieces of textual evidence that support an inference in informational text.		3 / Short answer	
Analyze the quality of textual evidence used to support an inference.			1 / Oral presentation

Source: Adapted from Marzano et al., 2016.
Source for standard: Archdiocese of Chicago, n.d.b.

Figure 5.1: Sample assessment blueprint.

In this plan, we can identify a number of choices the teacher has made. First, she has separated the two elements of score 2.0 content—vocabulary and simpler content and skills—into two learning targets that will be assessed with different questions. She has chosen to do this because of the nature of the content: vocabulary can be assessed with a very different kind of question than, for example, citing evidence. It is not always necessary to do this, but in this case, the teacher has appropriately chosen to separate them.

Next, notice that there are different kinds of questions for different kinds of content and scale levels because the teacher has aligned the item types with the content or skill that is being assessed. For students to demonstrate understanding of the simpler content at the score 2.0 level, matching works well with vocabulary, but short answer is more aligned to students' explaining citing evidence for what a text says explicitly. This remains true at the score 3.0 level, where the learning target requires citation but will also need explanation to ensure that the student understands the link between the textual inference and the evidence. Finally, analyzing the quality of evidence at score 4.0 requires a much deeper explanation to verify that the student's analysis goes beyond the expectation at score 3.0. While this could be handled in a traditional essay question, the teacher in this case has chosen to have students prepare and deliver a presentation. At every level, the learning target determines the type of assessment item, rather than the teacher selecting an item type and making it fit a learning target.

Individual classroom teachers, in planning and creating assessments for their classrooms, are unlikely to need to complete an assessment blueprint form for every single assessment. But the planning process this form provides is important practice in creating an assessment that is aligned to the learning targets that are being assessed. Thinking through the assessment in this way ensures the *validity* of the assessment—that the assessment measures what it is intended to measure. Further, aligning an assessment with the relevant scale is an important step in making sure that the assessment is fair. It will assess what students are being taught, with assessment items that are at an appropriate level.

To further explain the differences between assessment items at each level of the scale, consider the following examples. First, a second-grade mathematics scale on comparing fractions: the plan is shown in a chart (figure 5.2, page 96), rather than the assessment blueprint, but the planning process for the assessment items is the same. In the case of the score 2.0 item, the teacher has chosen a simple question that requires a one-word response. The answer is either correct or incorrect. This question is aligned to the cognitive demand of the learning target at score 2.0, simple recall of vocabulary. For the score 3.0 item, the student is required to meet the cognitive demand of the learning target, to compare two fractions with different denominators, and justify that comparison. At score 4.0, the cognitive demand again aligns to the learning target where the student must compare three fractions with different numerators and denominators. Note also that the student must explain his or her thinking.

As a final example, consider a set of assessment items for the secondary social studies standard, "Explain the relationship among cultural, social, economic, political, and technological features of early civilizations." The standard is not assigned to a single grade level; social studies standards are often generalized or assigned to grade bands at the secondary level, allowing schools and districts to assign the grade level based on local considerations. This standard is likely a middle-school-level standard. Figure 5.3 (page 96) shows the learning targets for each level of the proficiency scale, which will be assessed with the associated assessment items. At each level, the assessment item meets the cognitive demand of the learning target. These items represent examples of assessment items at each level, not a comprehensive group of assessment items that would sufficiently assess the learning targets at each level. For example, at score 3.0, the assessment item addresses only part of the learning target (culture and economics). Additional score 2.0 and score 3.0 assessment items would be needed to completely assess each learning target at those levels.

The following sections provide further information about which item types are usually best matched to each scale level.

Proficiency Scale Level	Learning Target	Aligned Assessment Item
2.0	The student will recall the meaning of the word *denominator*.	Does the word *denominator* refer to the top or bottom number on a fraction?
3.0	The student will justify the comparison of two fractions with different denominators.	Determine whether the correct symbols have been chosen to compare the two fractions. Then, explain why you made your choice. $\frac{4}{8} > \frac{5}{6}$ $\frac{1}{5} < \frac{1}{3}$
4.0	The student will order three fractions with different numerators and denominators and explain the process he or she used.	Order the following three fractions from least to greatest. Then, explain how you made your decision. $\frac{6}{8}$ $\frac{4}{9}$ $\frac{5}{10}$

Figure 5.2: Sample assessment items for grade 2 mathematics.

Proficiency Scale Level	Learning Target	Aligned Assessment Item
2.0	The student will recognize or recall specific vocabulary such as *aristocracy, Bronze Age, Iron Age, megalith, metallurgy, patriarchy*.	Does *patriarchy* refer to rule by the wealthy class?
2.0	The student will describe environmental conditions that influenced the development of early civilizations (for example, the prevailing wind, current, and flooding pattern in the Tigris-Euphrates, Nile, Indus, and Huang He river valleys).	What are the two most important environmental conditions that influenced the development of the early civilization of the Tigris-Euphrates river valley?
3.0	The student will explain the relationship among the cultural, social, economic, political, and technological features of early civilizations.	In an essay, explain the relationship between the cultural and economic features of early civilizations.
4.0	The student will compare the relationships among the cultural, social, economic, political, and technological features of early civilizations.	In an essay, determine which was a more powerful influence on the development of early civilizations: culture, social forces, economy, politics, or technology. Be sure to address each one.

Figure 5.3: Sample assessment items for secondary social studies.

Score 2.0 Items

Because the content found in the score 2.0 learning targets represents simpler knowledge and skills, the type of question should align with that kind of content. The teacher will want to be aware of the learning target's demands in choosing how to assess the student at this level. For example, if the learning target requires the student to recognize or recall certain vocabulary terms, the teacher might choose a multiple-choice question where the student chooses the correct term to match a given definition, or a matching item that lists a series of definitions and terms for the student to match. A more complex question that requires the application of those terms with an explanation of how they are applied would be beyond the score 2.0 learning target. Thus, score 2.0 assessment items typically take the form of multiple choice, matching, alternative choice, true/false, fill-in-the-blank, or multiple response (student provides two or more correct answers; Marzano et al., 2016). However, the teacher should choose what is most appropriate for the particular assessment situation.

Score 3.0 Items

At score 3.0, assessment items require students to respond at the level of the standard. This will mean more rigorous levels of thinking, and the type of assessment item will reflect that. Again, the first step is to review what is required by the learning target. As we discussed when aligning instructional strategies to learning targets, determining the cognitive demand of a learning target means reviewing not only the verb in the learning target but also the context of that verb. In the case of score 3.0, more elaborate student responses are often required by the verb and its context in the learning target, so short written response, essay, oral presentation, or projects work well (Marzano et al., 2016).

A good example of the importance of context is the score 3.0 learning target in the citing textual evidence scale (see figure 4.6, page 82): "Cite several pieces of textual evidence that support an inference in informational text." This learning target requires students to cite evidence, but the context includes a grade-level text that students will be examining, and supporting an inference in the text. The context here requires students to explain in some detail, drawing connections between the evidence they have cited and the inference being supported. Context has changed the cognitive demand, and it will change how the student can be assessed on this learning target. Here, a short-answer assessment item will serve well. Clearly, a text will be provided, and students will need to work through the evidence therein, identifying which points support an inference. Students would then explain the connection in a short (three to four sentences) answer.

You might question whether this learning target could not be assessed with a series of multiple-choice questions. The teacher might provide a text, then provide an inference, and ask students to select the piece of evidence that best supports the given inference. While this assesses whether the student can identify evidence that is valid support for an inference, such questions do not assess whether the students can *cite* evidence, which implies the process of accurately identifying that evidence.

Score 4.0 Items

Before discussing the types of assessment items a teacher might use at score 4.0, we must discuss the unique qualities of score 4.0 learning targets. As mentioned previously, score 4.0 on the proficiency scale is fundamentally different from scores 2.0 and 3.0 in that it does not include specific academic content that will be directly taught. The score 4.0 text includes an example of a score 4.0 task, but importantly indicates that score 4.0 performance is not limited to that specific activity. This has important implications for designing assessment items for score 4.0. Teachers can design assessment items based on the example provided on the proficiency scale, but they are not required to do so—the 4.0 item may take another form or use a different experience or activity, as long as it matches the cognitive demand. For this reason, as teachers begin to work with proficiency scales and aligned assessments, score 4.0 can often be challenging.

Score 4.0, in the generic learning target of "In addition to score 3.0, in-depth inferences and applications that go beyond what was taught," requires that students generate new thinking or apply their knowledge (the score 3.0 content) in unique and novel situations. After teachers have worked with the scale for several instructional cycles, this determination becomes easier, and for this reason, we recommend that teachers focus on the examples in the proficiency scale when first designing activities and assessments at this level.

As with score 3.0, the learning target examples (the verb and the context of the verb) will determine the type of assessment item. Because score 4.0 requires students to apply their understanding of score 3.0 content in a new way, one which has not been encountered in class instruction, score 4.0 assessment items take similar forms as score 3.0 items (short written response, essay, oral response, projects, presentation, and so on; Marzano et al., 2016).

Scores Based on Proficiency Scales

Assessments designed based on proficiency scales should also be scored according to the scale. In evaluating a student's performance on such an assessment, the teacher analyzes the pattern of performance in each leveled section of the assessment. Consider the pattern depicted in figure 5.4. This student answered all the score 2.0 items correctly, so the teacher can be confident that he clearly knows the content at score 2.0. His performance at 3.0 is less clear. He has had some success with these learning targets but seems to need some additional work. The student is not capable of score 4.0 performance on this assessment. Thus, the teacher would likely assign an overall score of 2.5 to this assessment. More important, this pattern of performance shows clearly what the student currently knows and what he has yet to master.

Scale Level	Number of Items	Items Answered Correctly
2.0	5	5
3.0	5	3
4.0	1	0

Figure 5.4: Sample assessment response pattern.

While leveled assessments readily lend themselves to interpreting student performance by scale level, not every instructional goal should be assessed with leveled questions. Indeed, some topics are better suited to a project or performance task rather than a set of leveled items. Examples of such alternative assessments are essays, physical education activities, fine arts performances, science labs, and the like. In these cases, the teacher provides students with the opportunity to create a performance or product that demonstrates ability on the priority standards for the instructional cycle. The teacher then uses the proficiency scale as a rubric to determine student performance along the learning progression. For example, consider the high school physical education scale in figure 5.5.

Learning Topic: The Four Components of Physical Fitness	
4.0	In addition to score 3.0, in-depth inferences and applications that go beyond what was taught in class Student performance *may* include, but is not limited to: • Student designs and implements a personal fitness program that includes the four components of physical fitness. The student monitors progress, analyzes the effectiveness of the program, and adjusts to increase the effectiveness of the program.

3.0	The student regularly participates in physical activities that promote and maintain the four components of physical fitness:
	
	   1. Muscular strength
	
	   2. Muscular endurance
	
	   3. Cardiovascular endurance
	
	   4. Flexibility

2.0	The student recognizes or recalls specific vocabulary such as: • *Muscular strength, muscular endurance, cardiovascular endurance, flexibility* The student performs basic processes such as: • Identify the four components of physical fitness. • Explain how a component of physical fitness is included in a particular physical activity.

Figure 5.5: Sample high school physical education scale.

Consider how a teacher would assess the learning target at score 3.0. Participation in such activities would be regularly observed by the physical education teacher. While there could be a specific assessment for the learning targets at score 2.0, and a separate one for score 4.0, the assessment of score 3.0 is ongoing. In this case, the teacher would use the scale as a rubric to determine whether the student consistently ("regularly") meets the standard and would assign a scale score to that performance. If the student does consistently meet the requirements of the target content, that score would be a 3.0. The proficiency scale, in delineating specific learning targets at each level, removes a great deal of the subjectivity typically associated with grading projects and performances.

Throughout the instructional cycle, teachers will assess student performances to monitor their increasing knowledge and ability on the learning targets. They will record these assessments and begin to assemble a body of evidence that reflects the learning students have demonstrated. This body of evidence will inform teacher decisions about the end-of-cycle status, or summative score, of the student. The summative score is the score the teacher assigns to the student after the instructional cycle is complete, and it reflects the end point where the student finished on the learning progression. Aligned assessment items make assigning the summative score easier for the teacher.

Student Goal Setting and Tracking

One of the most important advantages of using a proficiency scale for planning and instruction is that students can set their own personal goals and track their progress on those goals. In addition to the fact that this practice has a strong research base as a highly effective strategy—according to Marzano (2010), 32-percentile-point gains in student achievement—having students set and track personal learning goals is an excellent method for connecting students with their own learning (Dotson, 2016; McMillan, 2019; Watkins, 2019). Students who are involved in the learning progression on a personal level are more likely to understand the relevance of classroom activities, assignments, and assessments. For this reason, we strongly urge teachers to adopt this technique when they move to standards-based learning. In our experience, it is one of the quickest ways to improve students' involvement in their own learning.

When teachers use this technique with students, there are some important considerations regarding the type of goals students create and track. Student goals should be academic in nature and should be directly connected to the proficiency scale in use in the instructional cycle. Further, Heflebower and her colleagues (2019) indicated that students should focus on mastery of the learning targets for the unit, rather than a goal that compares their own performance with other students in the classroom. Comparative goals are those such as "I will be one of the most successful students in the classroom" or "I want to be one of the students who achieves 3.0." A mastery-orientated goal might sound like "I will increase my ability to create strong introductory paragraphs in my writing." It is academically focused on mastering a specific learning target from the instructional cycle proficiency scale. Further, because that learning target will be assessed with aligned assessments during the current instructional cycle, the student will get regular specific feedback on how he or she is doing in accomplishing the goal. Further information about the specifics of student goals and goal setting can be found in *A Teacher's Guide to Standards-Based Learning* (Heflebower et al., 2019).

We must acknowledge that the practice of having students set personal goals and track progress is time intensive. However, the payoff in increased student achievement and engagement is considerable. Because the strategy requires substantial class time, we recommend that teachers have students set and track personal goals on only a few priority standards. Typically, having students set academic goals requires thirty to sixty minutes of class time, and regular progress checks take fifteen to twenty minutes. Thus, selecting only a few learning targets on which to write goals to keep the process doable in terms of instructional time available is an important issue in planning. We recommend no more than three student goals per class or content area at any one time at the secondary level, no more than two at a time at the upper elementary level, and perhaps only a single goal in the primary grades.

Further, this strategy requires the teacher's commitment, not only in terms of devoting instructional time but also in terms of honoring its importance. If students believe the teacher considers goal setting important, they will be more likely to seriously engage with the practice. Teachers can send the message of the importance of goals by regularly referring to proficiency scales and reminding students that they have personal goals aligned to these scales, by modeling goal setting with students, and by modeling how to process feedback on the goals during the instructional cycle.

Students will need a method of setting and tracking goals in the form of a chart, graphic, or other progress form. When initiating the routine of goal setting and tracking progress with students, hold a classwide discussion of what makes a good, realistic goal. Students should consider the amount of time the class will spend on the current instructional cycle, how much progress is expected for the whole class (everyone will be expected to attain score 3.0), and their own strengths and challenges with the particular learning target. Once all of these elements are in place, teachers can provide the opportunity for students to set and track personal learning goals.

The process of setting goals begins with a preassessment aligned to the standards and scales for the upcoming instructional cycle. Students need to know where they are starting on the learning progression. The teacher scores the preassessment and provides each student with a score based on the proficiency scale. Students should understand that the preassessment score is not one that will appear in the gradebook; it is merely to determine a starting point for learning. It is perfectly acceptable to score at the lower levels of the scale early in the instructional cycle before much teaching and learning has occurred. Growth will come. The teacher should also share the proficiency scale for the instructional cycle with students so they understand the learning progression as a whole and each level of the scale. On the seventh-grade ELA instructional cycle plan we have been following, a good opportunity to do such goal setting would present itself on either day 2 or day 3. In the instructional cycle plan (figure 4.8, page 89), the preassessment for the cycle's proficiency scale is given on day 1; the teacher will need time to score that preassessment so students have the score as part of the goal-setting activity.

The proficiency scale provides clear levels of performance on the learning progression, and teachers provide instruction and assessment based on the scale, so a goal in that same format aligns with the work ahead. Thus, students can identify a level on the proficiency scale they intend to reach by a certain date: "By November 15, I will achieve 3.0 on the proficiency scale." Provide students with a timeline for accomplishing their goal—perhaps the instructional cycle, a semester, or an entire year—based on how long the learning target or standard for which the students are setting the goal will be operational. This will vary according to the grade level and sophistication of the student. Primary students may benefit from short-term goals, and secondary students may be able to handle semester- or year-long goals. Teachers should use their best judgment about the term of student-created personal goals.

As students progress toward their goals and track that progress, they need a way of organizing information, including assessment data. A form like the one in figure 5.6 (page 102) is an effective way of doing this. With this form, a student records the title or topic of each assessment related to the standard, and then fills in the boxes up to his or her score on that assessment, creating a bar chart of scores over time.

Name: _____

Priority Standard: _____

_____

Current Score (out of 4): _____   Goal: _____ by _____ (date)

In order to accomplish the above goal, I will do the following:

_____

_____

_____

_____

Goal Tracking

	A	B	C	D	E	F	G	H
4.0								
3.0								
2.0								
1.0								
0.0								

Assessments

A. _____ B. _____ C. _____ D. _____

E. _____ F. _____ G. _____ H. _____

Figure 5.6: Goal-setting and tracking form.

*Visit **MarzanoResources.com/reproducibles** for a free reproducible version of this figure.*

This form is designed for use with high school students. As mentioned previously, elementary teachers can use a simpler or friendlier version. Including appealing graphics as a format for the student to track progress, such as adding scoops to an ice-cream cone or taking steps up a mountain, accomplishes the same effect as the graph in figure 5.6, but in a more visually engaging format.

An important part of the tracking form is the prompt, "In order to accomplish the above goal, I will do the following." Here, students record the actions they will take to reach their personal goals. Once again, when first instituting this practice, the teacher must impart to students that they are making a personal commitment to go above and beyond what is normally required. A classwide discussion of the kinds of strategies that will pay off for the specific learning progression at hand will be vital each time goals are set. For example, if fourth graders are working on a mathematics goal around comparing fractions, one student might set a goal that reads, "I will be able to accurately compare fractions with different numerators and denominators." To accomplish this goal, the student decides additional practice might pay off in gaining fluency with the process at each level of the scale. In a secondary ELA classroom where students are working on a proficiency scale about analyzing literature, one student might plan to get involved more frequently in class discussions of grade-level texts to help achieve the goal of accurately analyzing literary texts. The efforts each student will undertake to meet or exceed his or her personal goal should be adjusted to the specific learning progression required by the proficiency scale.

Each time an aligned assessment provides additional data on student progress, each student should record that information on his or her tracking form. As stated previously, having some form of graphic representation of their progress helps students understand the importance of the data. A line or bar graph can do this very well. Students who see their line heading upward have their hard work reinforced. If the line begins to descend, an opportunity arises for the teacher and student to discuss changes to the student's own learning plan to turn his or her progress in the right direction. Inevitably, there will be students whose progress does not reflect the goal they have established. To prevent students from losing enthusiasm, teachers should provide opportunities to review progress regularly and often. In this way, students can identify and deal with problems before they become long-term patterns. When students see that there are ways to respond to slower-than-expected growth, they will bring problems forward sooner, with an attitude that helps them move toward success (McMillan, 2019).

When establishing and tracking their personal goals, students should have a way to easily access them during class. If students are responsible and maintain academic notebooks, the goal-tracking form can reside there. In many cases, especially with younger students, a folder in the classroom that the teacher maintains is more effective. Because goals need to be accessed often, the goal-tracking form must be available at all times—not only when students remember to bring it. That being said, in our experience, once students understand the importance and power of setting and tracking personal goals, they are more likely to bring and to maintain their goal sheets.

Some teachers also provide a method of tracking student progress on a public display in the classroom. Such public displays do not need to reveal individual progress by name. Teachers can assign a symbol or a number for each student so the progress is apparent, but each student's performance remains private information. We recommend teachers use their best judgment about doing this; some classes may find the public display problematic, and teachers are always the best judges of what will work with their students. Our experience is that the standards-based classroom readily becomes a learning community, with students often voluntarily sharing their own performance with other students, and students approaching overall class performance in a noncompetitive way. When students are measured on their progress on standards, rather than progress in comparison to each other, we've found they are more mutually supportive about academic performance. Again, the individual teacher is the best judge in this area.

Figures 5.7 (page 104) and 5.8 (page 104) show examples of such displays. In figure 5.7, each student has a strip of paper with a number, which is placed in a pocket indicating the current status on the learning progression. In figure 5.8, each student has a sticker with a number indicating the same kind of progress. Variations on this format are innumerable, but do not underestimate the power of such a display. With a proficiency scale, aligned assessments, and goals, that desired improvement is possible and clearly in the student's control!

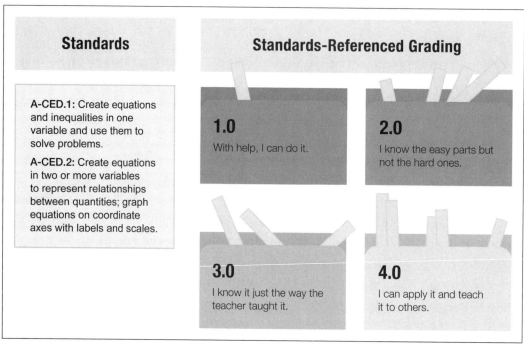

Source for standards: NGA & CCSSO, 2010b.

Figure 5.7: High school algebra classroom learning progression display.

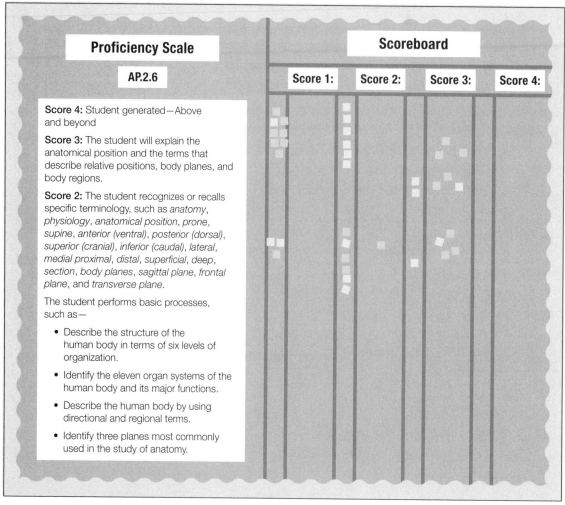

Source for standard: Colorado Career and Technical Education, n.d.

Figure 5.8: High school anatomy and physiology classroom learning progression display.

Summary

This chapter reviewed important considerations related to standards-based assessment, scoring, and progress. Assessments should be aligned to the learning progression defined by the associated proficiency scale. That way, teachers can score students' work according to the scale, communicating clear and consistent feedback. Students then track their own progress toward personal learning goals. The idea of involving students more deeply in their learning continues in the next chapter as we discuss the proficiency scale as a communication tool.

6

Communication Using Proficiency Scales

As we have shown throughout this book, proficiency scales are informational tools designed to support teachers in clarifying what to teach, aligning instruction and classroom assessments, and giving quality feedback to students. In turn, proficiency scales help students understand what they are learning, what constitutes proficiency, and how to track their progress, making the scales essential for students to take ownership of their learning. Because scales serve all these purposes, they are also an important and helpful tool for communicating about the learning process. Scales form the foundation for communication with students as well as with parents. In this chapter, we address the following topics.

- Communicating with students throughout the instructional cycle
- Bringing parents along on the learning progression
- Building relationships around the change to standards-based learning

Communicating With Students Throughout the Instructional Cycle

One tenet of standards-based learning is that student learning is central to what occurs in the classroom. It follows that good communication with students is an integral part of a student-centered approach. Fortunately, the use of proficiency scales facilitates communication with students. Students who understand clearly what they need to know and be able to do to succeed in class will be able to discuss their learning progress in a more objective way. The agreed-on set of learning targets provides the common language for teachers and students (and their parents) to discuss learning. For instance, when the COVID-19 pandemic caused many schools to quickly move to online formats, schools that provided proficiency scales for students and parents more clearly communicated the expectations. There was less wondering, "What is my student learning?" "How can I help my child learn the concepts?" "What is the level of proficiency expected?" Rather, proficiency scales provided a clearer communication between school and home.

Proficiency scales can be highly effective in reducing emotional reactions students may have during the journey to proficiency. It seems obvious that students may be frustrated when they do not know what the teacher expects. That anxiety can in turn cause undue stress for students and parents alike. In 1971, Mary Alice White described that when students don't know what they are learning or where all the activities are headed, it is analogous to an adult "sailing across an unknown sea, to an unknown destination" (as cited in Wiliam, 2018, p. 57). A number of studies have emphasized the significance of students clearly understanding what they are learning (Gray & Tall, 1994; Sadler, 1989; White & Frederiksen, 1998; Wiliam, 2018). Additionally, when students set and track personal goals based on the learning targets in a proficiency scale, they are closely connected with their own learning and thus tend to be more invested in it. As Chase Nordengren (2019) stated:

> Goal setting—one of the many forms of student-involved data use (Jimerson & Reames, 2015)—gets students involved in reviewing their assessment results, working with their teachers to set reasonable but aspirational goals for improvement, and continuing to drive their learning with frequent reference to those goals.

Proficiency scales can also make learning more achievable. Students may initially see the journey to proficiency as an enormous leap; the use of a proficiency scale allows teachers to discuss incremental goals that make the task seem less daunting. Also, when students see examples of work at each level of the scale and the growth from one product to another, they can appreciate that the goal is not to achieve proficiency all at once. Many students believe that people are either born skilled and "smart" or not; they do not believe that hard work can change their potential for success (Dweck, 2006). Small, incremental growth through the levels of the proficiency scale helps teachers change those mindsets in students. This likely even affects student achievement. One study found that early success led to increased subsequent success, in comparison to those who did not experience success early on (van de Rijt, Kang, Restivo, & Patil, 2014).

Some teachers create proficiency scales that measure students' work habits. For instance, they may have proficiency scales that measure behavior skills like following directions, turning in work on time, effort, and the like. This way, teachers can give feedback about those important life skills. Figure 6.1 displays a sample proficiency scale for effort and preparation.

Score	Behavior Description
4.0	I am working very hard and preparing even more than I think may be necessary to achieve proficiency.
3.0	I am trying hard enough to accomplish my goal of proficiency.
2.0	Even though I am trying, it is not enough to achieve proficiency.
1.0	I am not trying very hard or preparing well.

Source: Adapted from Marzano & Pickering, 2011.

Figure 6.1: Sample scale for effort and preparation.

Teachers may have students rate themselves and directly compare the effect of their effort on academic success. In this way, students can see the direct connection between effort and academic performance. Imagine a teacher uses a graph similar to the one in figure 6.2 to have students track their academic progress with one line, while using another to rate their effort and preparation. Note that the student's effort and achievement match at first, then diverge, but rebound in concert later. This type of tracking provides discussion and goal-setting opportunities between the teacher and student. The teacher might ask, "What did you do differently in your effort and preparation this week that you didn't do last week?" "What did you find works well for you?" "What will you keep doing?" "Where do you need support or ideas from me?"

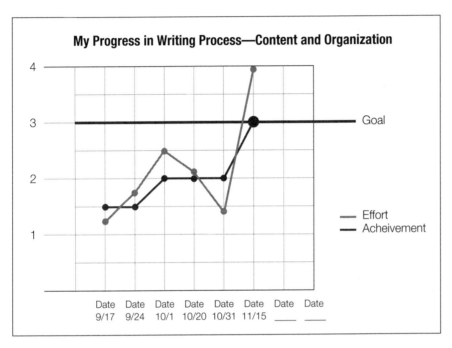

Figure 6.2: Student progress tracking for achievement and effort.

As teachers become more familiar with the use of proficiency scales in the classroom, many additional uses will become apparent, such as tracking progress, setting goals, and communicating progress to parents. Perhaps the most important effect of the scale and students' connection to the learning progression it represents, however, is the change in attitude toward learning that students exhibit. In our experience in standards-based classrooms, students are often more eager to learn, less apprehensive about assessments, and more likely to accept personal responsibility for their own learning.

Bringing Parents Along on the Learning Progression

One topic we haven't yet discussed is parents and guardians, and how proficiency scales can be helpful for them. Proficiency scales communicate how their children are progressing, what they still need to master, and what they need to know and do to be successful in class. As mentioned previously, scales can be useful in online and hybrid learning formats for helping parents understand what their child needs to learn and what specific learning targets signify proficiency. This simple act of clarity puts teachers, students, and parents on the same team. Traditional education can sometimes feel like a guessing game controlled by the teacher—guess what you will learn today, guess what I put on the test, guess how you scored. Withholding information fosters a culture of blame and pits parents against teachers. Parents may think or say, "Why wasn't the teacher clear with my child?" or "Why didn't the teacher help my child do better?" Proficiency scales bring a stop to these recriminations by giving parents a window into the teaching and learning processes. When students and parents clearly understand expectations, there is less adversity between school and home and less disparity between families who feel comfortable navigating the school system and helping their children with schoolwork and those who do not. In the following sections, we discuss how these tools enhance common school-home interactions.

Back-to-School Nights

Proficiency scales can profoundly change parent-teacher interactions like back-to-school nights. During back-to-school nights, many parents (especially those of secondary students) find themselves scrambling through their child's schedule, merely hoping to find the right room, inundated with numerous syllabi and vague explanations of different teachers' content and expectations. By the end of the night, it's a miracle if they've retained any information at all.

What if instead teachers presented a minilesson to parents about what a proficiency scale is, how it will be used in that class, and how it will help parents monitor their children's learning? Parents would likely better understand what proficiency scales are, how they will be used, and how they will inform students and teachers. It will provide a clear picture for how to be successful in the grade-level content or course. To introduce the concept, a teacher might share a sample scale related to a skill such as making a bed or unloading the dishwasher—something to which virtually all parents can relate. Figure 6.3 shows a humorous proficiency scale for the skill of making a bed.

Scale Score	Making a Bed
4.0	You not only made your bed perfectly as described at score 3.0, but also taught others how to make their beds!
3.0	Your bed has sheets, blanket, and comforter in the right order. There are no wrinkles in the comforter. Pillows are fluffed and placed carefully at the head of the bed. You cannot see the top sheet hanging out below the blanket.
2.0	Your comforter has many wrinkles and bumps. The blanket is bunched up under it, and your top sheet is hanging out below.
1.0	Your bed is as you left it. There is no attempt at making it.

Figure 6.3: Sample scale for making a bed.

Then, the teacher can provide the proficiency scales for the first unit of study and explain how both instruction and assessments would connect to them. We posit this is a much more edifying and valuable use of parents' time than the typical back-to-school night. We have used this approach ourselves and talked to many other teachers who have as well. Rather than parents pretending to listen to a teacher presenting a list of rules and books used in a class, families act like a class. The teacher teaches what a proficiency scale is, how it is helpful, and how it will be used in various content areas throughout the year. She models a five- to seven-minute minilesson—even with a quiz at the end!

Parent-Teacher and Student-Led Conferences

Proficiency scales can also lend specificity to conversations with parents about their children's learning. Using scales during conferences has several benefits. First, it focuses conversations on the knowledge and skills students are developing. Many parents are accustomed to grading systems that compare and rank students rather than chart each individual student's current status and growth. They may ask, "How is my child doing relative to others?" In our experience, parents sometimes use such comparisons as a barometer for themselves as parents. Although you want to allay any fears, the goal in standards-based learning is that *all* students reach proficiency. They may simply need more or less time and support. It is less about comparison and more about competency. A teacher may start by sharing a sample priority standard with parents—one to be mastered by the end of the year. This may involve explaining how standards may look and feel different from how parents were taught directly from textbooks, with students progressing through the book hoping to master components and moving on, often never to see those components again. Then, the teacher can go on to share what a typical unit will be like and when there will be assessment opportunities throughout to gauge where students are in their proficiency. Finally, the teacher might express what he or she will do for reteaching and reassessment opportunities throughout the unit or even the year to ensure that students have multiple opportunities to relearn and master the priority standards and proficiency scales.

Second, centering the conversation on the proficiency scale limits the grade negotiation that can sometimes accompany conferences: "What extra credit can my son do to raise his grade?" "How can my daughter pass this class?" Teachers often refer to this as *point-grabbing*. Some parents (and some students) may care more about what grade a student has than what learning occurs. The proficiency scale makes it clear that grades are not an accumulation of points but a reflection of learning. Educators must retrain parents (and students) to understand that modern standards are complex and often span an entire year. If the class has only addressed the simpler content for a topic early on in a quarter or trimester, a score of 2.0 is a more accurate representation of a student's current learning than a misleading A grade. Mastering complex content and skills takes time and development.

Finally, scales may help put an end to personalization in conference discussions. In some cases, teachers may receive blame from parents: "My son just doesn't learn well from you." "My daughter is doing well in all her *other* classes." When personal criticism ensues, learning is the victim. The conversation about learning is hijacked by comments about personality traits, speed of instruction, unfair expectations, and the like. Proficiency scales are consistent and objective, and keep the conversation concentrated on learning. When teachers reference proficiency scales and the evidence a student has provided in relation to them, the facts speak for themselves. It takes away the subjectivity that parents (and students) have become accustomed to seeing and hearing: This teacher wants you to speak a lot in class; another doesn't care. One teacher gives bonus points for things unrelated to learning (bringing in supplies or signing syllabi); another expects you to teach yourself outside of class. One teacher is an "easy grader," and another hardly ever gives As. Achieving in school has previously been more about teacher-pleasing than learning key concepts to proficient levels. When teachers clearly articulate expectations and evidence, along with opportunities for reteaching and reassessment, parents and students appreciate the opportunity for *all* students to learn and succeed, not just a select few. Less competition means more learning for more students.

Even better than parent-teacher conferences based on proficiency scales are student-led conferences based on scales. Just as the term suggests, students (not teachers) lead conversations about their own learning—their successes, struggles, and goals toward achievement. Teachers support and answer questions as needed, but ultimately students share their learning journey with their parents. Students are very familiar with the set of scales used in class, and they can use those as the foundation of a conversation with their parents or guardians. Rather than a display of projects or other classwork that the student is proud of, a conference based on scales is a conversation about student achievement and progress. Scales also provide a basis for students to set learning goals and share them with their parents. Conferencing becomes less about sharing the work and more about sharing the learning.

Student-led conferences are often organized somewhat like parent-teacher conferences, with short appointments for each family to meet with the teacher. For elementary school students, this may still be the best approach. For middle and high school, however, since the main goal is for students to talk with their parents, let us offer an alternative process for consideration. The following steps allow a team of teachers to host student-led conferences for all their students at once.

1. In advance of the conference, have students collect a folder of materials. These materials should include:

    a. Two or three required proficiency scales and one or two scales of the student's choice (younger students might have three to five scales in total, while older students may have this number for each subject)

    b. Previously evaluated assessments that correspond to each proficiency scale in the folder

    c. Three learning targets for which the student is proficient within that course and one or two learning targets he or she is still working toward

2. Set up the conference area with tables. Ensure there is enough space for all students who are scheduled to attend (you can stagger arrivals or hold multiple sessions if needed). It is best if there are enough tables for each family to have its own table for privacy. Yet, larger tables can accommodate two families. On each table is a set of different-colored flags or other signals, as well as a cup or stand to hold the flags upright when needed. Each flag color represents a content area—for example, blue might be for mathematics, pink for physical education, green for science, and so forth.

3. Students bring or retrieve their course folders and, with their parents, seat themselves at a table. The teachers mingle around the conference area

greeting students and parents, while waiting to see if they are needed for specific discussions.

4. Students share their learning with their parents, using the documents in their folders to guide the conversation. If and when a student and his or her parents have a question, they place the appropriate flag into the cup or stand. This way, the respective teacher will see the flag and approach the table for discussion. After answering the question, the teacher returns the flag to the table.

This process is repeated throughout the timeframe in which students and parents hold their conferences. Some students and parents may use the flags often, some not at all. Using this process, no one is rushed for time, allotted a too-brief appointment slot, or required to speak with every content-area teacher. The pacing is controlled by students and parents. If space or teacher availability is a concern, you can schedule staggered times or multiple sessions, perhaps assigning students to sessions by last name. The goal is to accommodate all students and parents when and how it works best. As a teacher, you know there are some parents with whom you don't need to meet because their children are progressing well. There are others with whom you would spend many minutes or even hours if time allowed! Here, time is allotted by need, not by requirement. If needed, parents may schedule an additional time with a teacher to discuss specific issues.

As an example of a student-led conference, imagine that a student and his parents arrive at their allotted time. They are greeted by a sign that welcomes them and presents the following instructions.

- Please collect your folders for your classes and find a place to sit to discuss your work.

- Work through each content-area folder one at a time.

- If you need help or want to speak with a specific teacher, place the appropriately labeled flag into the cup. That teacher will come to you.

- When you are finished, please place your folders back in the crates.

- Have a great day!

This is but one process for student-led conferences. There are a myriad of approaches and systems. The key is that *students* are visiting with their parents about their learning, because *students* are really the only ones who can do something about their own learning.

If you select a more traditional parent-teacher conference, proficiency scales can still be an integral part. For example, a teacher using a traditional conferencing format will bring out the proficiency scales for a content area. The teacher will show the parents and explain the level at which their child is currently achieving. Often, a teacher will accompany this discussion with samples of tests and assignments that exemplify the proficiency scale score. Whatever the format, be certain that conversations are centered around the student's current level of proficiency on priority standards. This can be done by the teacher with parents, or by the student with parents as the teacher looks on.

At-Home Learning Experiences

Proficiency scales can enable parents to better support their children's learning at home. When parents comprehend the learning target and progression, they can help locate resources, support online learning experiences, and even create learning opportunities during everyday household experiences. As previously mentioned, this was especially important in the online and hybrid learning environments many families encountered during the COVID-19 pandemic, when parents were desperate for exactly the type of clarity that proficiency scales provide.

All parents want their children to be successful, regardless of socioeconomic status, living conditions, or family structure. Schools and parents' working in concert helps students. Providing clear expectations and information to parents makes this guidance easier within any living situation. It is useful for grandparents raising grandchildren, childcare facilities supporting students with homework, students working in isolation, and families where parents are integrally involved. Clearly communicating expectations helps all students (no matter their home situation) with greater opportunities for achieving success.

Here's an example from one of the authors' experiences with her son, Nate. When Nate was in fifth grade, he was struggling with how to add and subtract decimals—a priority standard he needed to master. As Nate's teacher thoughtfully had him reflect on his learning during class and the evidence he needed to provide for his level of proficiency, it was clear that Nate wasn't yet adept with adding and subtracting decimals. The teacher had Nate use a set of highlighters to color-code the knowledge and skills he'd mastered, those he was working on, and those still beyond his development at that time. Then, Nate's teacher insightfully included the relevant proficiency scales in Nate's Friday folder—a folder used to send homework and other documents home over the weekend. In Nate's busy family, Friday folders were more of a Sunday evening scramble. One of Nate's parents would quickly scan the documents included for items that needed parental signatures— permission slips, reading records, and so on. Yet, when proficiency scales appeared in the folder, the entire process changed.

As Nate arrived home, he asked his parents to sit down to review his Friday folder. To his parents' surprise, Nate extracted the proficiency scale and shared with his parents his highlighting system. They noted not only what was being taught, but also how Nate was progressing with it. When his mother saw his lack of proficiency in adding and subtracting decimals, a lesson ensued. She planned for Nate to accompany her the next morning to the grocery store. She was thinking about how she could have him practice his skills of adding and subtracting decimals during a routine grocery shopping trip. Instead of having Nate help organize the cart or run for a specific product, she instead gave him an adding and subtracting decimals task. She put Nate in charge of getting butter. She gave the direction to get packages of butter that were neither the least expensive nor the most expensive in the dairy case. It took Nate a while, but he returned with a few options. He and his mother had a minilesson about adding and subtracting decimals to determine the difference in prices. One package cost $5.59 and another $3.29; Nate subtracted decimals to determine that one container of butter was $2.30 more than the other. Normally, getting groceries didn't turn into a lesson. Yet, because Nate's parents clearly knew what he needed to practice in math, they could incorporate that practice into this everyday endeavor. In addition, Nate's mother helped him appreciate a real-life situation where adding and subtracting decimals were paramount to staying within a grocery budget.

Building Relationships Around the Change to Standards-Based Learning

As students and parents see proficiency scales as the means to an end, more support for standards-based learning results. They recognize that learning is a journey and the proficiency scales exemplify that progression of learning. When educators continue to emphasize the importance of learning over the importance of achieving a score on possibly unrelated assignments or assessments, school becomes less about competition for a top score, a designation of valedictorian, or the sorting of winners and losers. Rather, it becomes an understanding that *all* students can and will be successful on priority standards, provided the time and supports they need. School becomes a place for collaboration, critical thinking, exploration, support for and with others, and the understanding that everyone can and will succeed. Make no mistake—this is not a participation-trophy system. Students must *earn* their achievement and do so through teachers' valid and reliable practices. Educators must be clear with *all* students about what is important to know and be able to do, how to achieve those goals, and what systems will support and extend the learning.

Learning a new system takes time. It may require schools and districts to communicate more than they have in the past. It may also mean that educators "sell" these ideas to build support. That simply means they share the rationale for the changes discussed in this resource and provide evidence for the successes they encounter. This type of change takes everyone. It cannot be left alone to a classroom teacher, a building leader, a district leader, or a parent to discover on his or her own. It must be collective. It must be universal and pervasive within your system. Share. Then, share some more. Earning trust takes evidence over time. This will not be fast, but it will be worth it. For more information about strategies and supports to build consensus, see *Leading Standards-Based Learning* (Heflebower et al., 2021).

Summary

In this final chapter, we discussed the use of proficiency scales as a communication tool. The scale is the center of conversation with students throughout the learning process. Further, by sharing the proficiency scale with parents and explaining the learning progression the scale represents, teachers can leverage parents' willingness to assist. At the very least, parents will be more familiar and supportive of teachers' efforts in standards-based learning if they understand how the system works for their children.

Epilogue

Adopting standards-based learning can be an exciting and motivating experience for teachers, whether you are new to the profession or an experienced veteran. It can mean higher levels of student achievement, higher levels of student engagement with their own learning, and, eventually, more efficient and meaningful teacher experiences. At the same time, the transition is challenging; it involves a shift in one's entire sense of what is happening in the classroom. The shift to planning and instructing with standards takes time, and everyone must move at his or her own pace. Be patient with your own progress, and keep in mind that the benefits outweigh the challenge you are facing.

Perhaps the most important benefit that teachers will encounter is the shift in classroom focus away from grades and toward learning. Students may be the first ones to understand this shift. One of this book's authors found that a student expressed his appreciation of the standards-based system by exclaiming, "It's about the learning!" For students who are used to seeing school as a game that requires them to balance action versus reward, standards-based learning can be a revelation, and it can represent a real shift in how students think about their own roles in the classroom. Students who see learning as the focus and who are provided with proficiency scales and aligned instruction and feedback can see their own learning increase, and often find a new enthusiasm for learning itself. And that provides a new enthusiasm for their teachers as well.

Another important benefit standards-based learning provides to students is a sense that they have some control over their own performance in the classroom. This can be inspiring for them, and with that inspiration comes a greater likelihood that students will become lifelong learners. Rather than a chore, something that must be done because the teacher insists on it, learning becomes something that has its own rewards, and students, observing their learning gradually increase in the classroom, often find that they make choices to continue that growth when their time in the classroom is over.

Teachers often report a refreshing change in their own approach to the classroom with standards-based learning. The alignment of curriculum, instruction, assessment, and feedback along with clearly defined standards means that the actions teachers take every day in the classroom make sense in new ways. The clarity that results can be re-energizing as well, and, coupled with a new enthusiasm about learning from students, the classroom often becomes the venue many teachers wish it could be—a place where the joy of learning prevails.

In the process of shifting to standards-based learning, teachers may find they confront long-held opinions and beliefs that might have to change. The change to standards-based learning is gradual, at the teacher's own pace, with the occasional pothole in the road. But the prospect of having standards-based learning fully functional in the classroom is just the goal. The journey is equally challenging and refreshing—a time to reenergize and adjust, to see students as capable and enthusiastic, to view this wonderful profession of education as an inspiring and worthwhile daily privilege once again! It has certainly been that for each of us. We hope you will accept the challenge of moving to standards-based learning in your classroom, and that in that shift the renewed enthusiasm for teaching happens for you, too.

References and Resources

Ainsworth, L. (2003). *Power standards: Identifying the standards that matter the most*. Denver, CO: Advanced Learning Press.

Alsalhi, N. R., Eltahir, M. E., & Al-Qatawneh, S. S. (2019). The effect of blended learning on the achievement of ninth grade students in science and their attitudes towards its use. *Heliyon*, *5*(9). Accessed at https://www.sciencedirect.com/science/article/pii/S2405844019360840 on June 4, 2021.

Archdiocese of Chicago. (n.d.a). *Benchmark report: English language arts grade 2*. Accessed at http://ocs.archchicago.org/Portals/23/Benchmarks%20ELA%202_1_1.pdf on July 12, 2021.

Archdiocese of Chicago. (n.d.b). *Benchmark report: English language arts grade 7*. Accessed at http://ocs.archchicago.org/Portals/23/Benchmarks%20ELA%207_1_1.pdf on July 12, 2021.

California Department of Education. (2020). *Historical and social sciences analysis skills*. Accessed at www.cde.ca.gov/be/st/ss/hssanalysisskills.asp on May 14, 2021.

Colorado Career and Technical Education. (n.d.). *Basic anatomy and physiology: Course standards*. Accessed at http://coloradostateplan.com/educator/health-science/health-science-courses/basic-anatomy-and-physiology-course-standards/ on July 12, 2021.

Colorado Department of Education. (2020). *Colorado academic standards online*. Accessed at www.cde.state.co.us/apps/standards/2,9,31 on May 14, 2021.

Conzemius, A. E., & O'Neill, J. (2014). *The handbook for SMART school teams: Revitalizing best practices for collaboration* (2nd ed.). Bloomington, IN: Solution Tree Press.

Corwin & SmartBrief. (2017). *How to empower student learning with teacher clarity* [White paper]. Accessed at https://us.corwin.com/sites/default/files/corwin_whitepaper_teacherclarity_may2017_final.pdf on January 26, 2021.

Council of Chief State School Officers. (2019). *Grade 7 English language arts/literacy end of year S/M informational text set*. Washington, DC: Author. Accessed at https://resources.newmeridiancorp.org/wp-content/uploads/2019/07/EOY-S-M-Hey-Saw_FINAL.pdf on May 28, 2021.

Dotson, R. (2016). Goal setting to increase student academic performance. *Journal of School Administration Research and Development*, *1*(1), 44–46.

Dweck, C. S. (2006). *Mindset: The new psychology of success*. New York: Random House.

Frechette, A. (2017). *The impact of a standards-based approach on student motivation* [Doctoral dissertation, University of New England]. DUNE: DigitalUNE. Accessed at https://dune.une.edu/theses/141 on June 4, 2021.

Gray, E. M., & Tall, D. O. (1994). Duality, ambiguity, and flexibility: A "proceptual" view of simple arithmetic. *Journal for Research in Mathematics Education, 25*(2), 116–140.

Guskey, T. R. (Ed.). (2009). *The teacher as assessment leader.* Bloomington, IN: Solution Tree Press.

Hattie, J. (2009). *Visible learning: A synthesis of over 800 meta-analyses relating to achievement.* London: Routledge.

Haystead, M. W. (2016). *An analysis of the relationship between English language arts and mathematics achievement and essential learning mastery in grades 3 and 4.* Centennial, CO: Marzano Resources. Accessed at https://www.marzanoresources.com/clark-pleasant-istep -ela-math-exec-summary.html on June 4, 2021.

Heflebower, T., Hoegh, J. K., & Warrick, P. B. (2014). *A school leader's guide to standards-based grading.* Bloomington, IN: Marzano Resources.

Heflebower, T., Hoegh, J. K., & Warrick, P. B. (2021). *Leading standards-based learning: An implementation guide for schools and districts.* Bloomington, IN: Marzano Resources.

Heflebower, T., Hoegh, J. K., Warrick, P. B., & Flygare, J. (2019). *A teacher's guide to standards-based learning.* Bloomington, IN: Marzano Resources.

Heinrich, C. J., Darling-Aduana, J., Good, A., & Cheng, H. (2019). A look inside online educational settings in high school: Promise and pitfalls for improving educational opportunities and outcomes. *American Educational Research Journal, 56*(6), 2147–2188.

Hoegh, J. K. (2020). *A handbook for developing and using proficiency scales in the classroom.* Bloomington, IN: Marzano Resources.

Iamarino, D. L. (2014). The benefits of standards-based grading: A critical evaluation of modern grading practices. *Current Issues in Education, 17*(2). Accessed at https://cie.asu .edu/ojs/index.php/cieatasu/article/view/1234 on June 4, 2021.

Marzano, R. J. (2003). *What works in schools: Translating research into action.* Alexandria, VA: Association for Supervision and Curriculum Development.

Marzano, R. J. (2006). *Classroom assessment and grading that work.* Alexandria, VA: Association for Supervision and Curriculum Development.

Marzano, R. J. (2009). *Designing and teaching learning goals and objectives.* Bloomington, IN: Marzano Resources.

Marzano, R. J. (2010). *Formative assessment and standards-based grading.* Bloomington, IN: Marzano Resources.

Marzano, R. J. (2017). *The new art and science of teaching.* Bloomington, IN: Solution Tree Press.

Marzano, R. J. (2018). *Making classroom assessments reliable and valid.* Bloomington, IN: Solution Tree Press.

Marzano, R. J. (2019). *The handbook for the new art and science of teaching.* Bloomington, IN: Solution Tree Press.

Marzano, R. J., Heflebower, T., Hoegh, J. K., Warrick, P. B., & Grift, G. (2016). *Collaborative teams that transform schools: The next step in PLCs.* Bloomington, IN: Marzano Resources.

Marzano, R. J., Norford, J. S., Finn, M., & Finn, D., III. (2017). *A handbook for personalized competency-based education.* Bloomington, IN: Marzano Resources.

Marzano, R. J., & Pickering, D. J. (2011). *The highly engaged classroom*. Bloomington, IN: Marzano Resources.

Marzano, R. J., Pickering, D. J., & Pollock, J. E. (2001). *Classroom instruction that works: Research-based strategies for increasing student achievement*. Alexandria, VA: Association for Supervision and Curriculum Development.

Marzano, R. J., Warrick, P. B., & Simms, J. A. (2014). *A handbook for High Reliability Schools: The next step in school reform*. Bloomington, IN: Marzano Resources.

Marzano, R. J., & Yanoski, D. C. (2016). *Proficiency scales for the new science standards: A framework for science instruction and assessment*. Bloomington, IN: Marzano Resources.

Marzano, R. J., Yanoski, D. C., Hoegh, J. K., & Simms, J. A. (2013). *Using Common Core standards to enhance classroom instruction and assessment*. Bloomington, IN: Marzano Resources.

Marzano Resources. (n.d.a). *The critical concepts*. Accessed at https://www.marzanoresources.com/educational-services/critical-concepts on September 11, 2020.

Marzano Resources. (n.d.b). *The Marzano compendium of instructional strategies*. Accessed at www.marzanoresources.com/online-compendium/intro on October 9, 2020.

McMillan, D. (2019). *What are the effects of goal-setting on motivation and academic achievement in a fourth grade classroom?* [Master's action research project, St. Catherine University]. Sophia. Accessed at https://sophia.stkate.edu/maed/337 on June 4, 2021.

Moeller, A. K., Theiler, J. M., & Wu, C. (2012). Goal setting and student achievement: A longitudinal study. *Faculty Publications: Department of Teaching, Learning and Teacher Education, 159*. Accessed at https://digitalcommons.unl.edu/cgi/viewcontent.cgi?article=1158&context=teachlearnfacpub on May 4, 2021.

National Center on Education and the Economy. (n.d.). *Canada*. Accessed at https://ncee.org/center-on-international-education-benchmarking/top-performing-countries/canada-overview/ on June 4, 2021.

National Governors Association Center for Best Practices & Council of Chief State School Officers. (2010a). *Common Core State Standards for English language arts and literacy in history/social studies, science, and technical subjects*. Washington, DC: Authors. Accessed at www.corestandards.org/assets/CCSSI_ELA%20Standards.pdf on April 7, 2021.

National Governors Association Center for Best Practices & Council of Chief State School Officers. (2010b). *Common Core State Standards for mathematics*. Washington, DC: Authors. Accessed at http://www.corestandards.org/wp-content/uploads/Math_Standards1.pdf on June 10, 2021.

Nevada Department of Education. (2014). *Employability skills for career readiness standards*. Carson City, NV: Author. Accessed at https://doe.nv.gov/uploadedFiles/ndedoenvgov/content/CTE/Documents/Employability-Skills-for-Career-Readiness-STDS-ADA.pdf on May 14, 2021.

NGSS Lead States. (2013). *Next Generation Science Standards: For states, by states*. Washington, DC: National Academies Press.

No Child Left Behind (NCLB) Act of 2001, Pub. L. No. 107-110, § 115, Stat. 1425 (2002).

Nordengren, C. (2019). *Goal-setting practices that support a learning culture*. Accessed at https://kappanonline.org/goal-setting-practices-support-learning-culture-nordengren/ on May 14, 2021.

North Dakota Department of Public Instruction. (2017). *North Dakota mathematics content standards: Grades K–12*. Accessed at https://www.nd.gov/dpi/sites/www/files/documents/Academic%20Support/v3.Mathematics%20Standards%20Final%208.14.17.pdf on July 12, 2021.

O'Connor, K. (2018). *How to grade for learning: Linking grades to standards* (4th ed.). Thousand Oaks, CA: Corwin Press.

Palloff, R. M., & Pratt, K. (2007). *Building online learning communities: Effective strategies for the virtual classroom* (2nd ed.). San Francisco: Jossey-Bass.

Porter, A., McMaken, J., Hwang, J., & Yang, R. (2011). Assessing the Common Core standards: Opportunities for improving measures of instruction. *Educational Researcher, 40*(4), 186–188.

Queen's Printer for Ontario. (n.d.a). *B1. Number sense*. Accessed at https://www.dcp.edu.gov.on.ca/en/curriculum/elementary-mathematics/grades/g4-math/strand-b/b1 on May 24, 2021.

Queen's Printer for Ontario. (n.d.b). *The mathematical processes*. Accessed at https://www.dcp.edu.gov.on.ca/en/curriculum/elementary-mathematics/context/the-mathematical-processes on May 24, 2021.

Queen's Printer for Ontario. (n.d.c). *The strands in the mathematics curriculum*. Accessed at https://www.dcp.edu.gov.on.ca/en/curriculum/elementary-mathematics/context/the-strands-in-the-mathematics-curriculum on July 20, 2021.

Sadler, D. R. (1989). Formative assessment and the design of instructional systems. *Instructional Science, 18*(2), 119–144.

Schimmer, T. (2016). *Grading from the inside out: Bringing accuracy to student assessment through a standards-based mindset*. Bloomington, IN: Solution Tree Press.

Simms, J. A. (2016). *The critical concepts (Final version: English language arts, mathematics, and science)*. Centennial, CO: Marzano Resources. Accessed at https://www.marzanoresources.com/the-critical-concepts.html on April 27, 2021.

van de Rijt, A., Kang, S. M., Restivo, M., & Patil, A. (2014). Field experiments of success-breeds-success dynamics. *Proceedings of the National Academy of Sciences, 111*(19), 6934–6939.

Watkins, V. (2019). *The effects of goal setting and data tracking on student performance* [Master's thesis, Northwestern College]. NWCommons. Accessed at https://nwcommons.nwciowa.edu/education_masters/121/ on June 3, 2021.

White, B. Y., & Frederiksen, J. R. (1998). Inquiry, modeling, and metacognition: Making science accessible to all students. *Cognition and Instruction, 16*(1), 3–118.

Wiliam, D. (2018). *Embedded formative assessment* (2nd ed.). Bloomington, IN: Solution Tree Press.

Woodward, C. V. (Ed.). (1981). *Mary Chesnut's Civil War*. New Haven, CT: Yale University Press.

Index

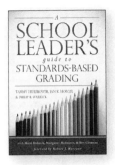

A School Leader's Guide to Standards-Based Grading
Tammy Heflebower, Jan K. Hoegh, and Philip B. Warrick
Assess and report student performance with standards-based grading rather than using traditional systems that incorporate nonacademic factors. Learn to assess and report performance based on prioritized standards, and gain effective strategies for offering students feedback on their progress.
BKL019

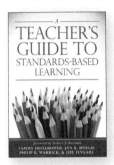

A Teacher's Guide to Standards-Based Learning
Tammy Heflebower, Jan K. Hoegh, Philip B. Warrick, and Jeff Flygare
Designed specifically for K–12 teachers, this resource details a sequential approach for adopting and implementing standards-based learning. The authors provide practical advice, real-world examples, and answers to frequently asked questions designed to support you through this important transition.
BKL044

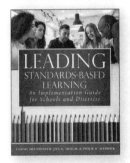

Leading Standards-Based Learning
Tammy Heflebower, Jan K. Hoegh, and Philip B. Warrick
Standards-based learning is a great step forward for schools, but it must be implemented correctly to ensure the best educational experience possible. In this comprehensive implementation guide, the authors outline a research-backed, five-phase plan for leading the transition to a standards-based system.
BKL052

A Handbook for Developing and Using Proficiency Scales in the Classroom
Jan K. Hoegh
Discover a clear path for creating and utilizing high-quality proficiency scales. Through this practical handbook, you will gain access to a comprehensive toolkit of strategies, methods, and examples for a variety of content areas and grade levels.
BKL045

The New Art and Science of Teaching
Robert J. Marzano
This title is a greatly expanded volume of the original *The Art and Science of Teaching*, offering a framework for substantive change based on Dr. Marzano's 50 years of education research. While the previous model focused on teacher outcomes, the new version places focus on student outcomes.
BKF776

MARZANO Resources

Visit MarzanoResources.com or call 888.849.0851 to order.

Professional Development Designed for Success

Empower your staff to tap into their full potential as educators. As an all-inclusive research-into-practice resource center, we are committed to helping your school or district become highly effective at preparing every student for his or her future.

Choose from our wide range of customized professional development opportunities for teachers, administrators, and district leaders. Each session offers hands-on support, personalized answers, and accessible strategies that can be put into practice immediately.

Bring Marzano Resources experts to your school for results-oriented training on:

- ▶ Assessment & Grading
- ▶ Curriculum
- ▶ Instruction
- ▶ School Leadership

- ▶ Teacher Effectiveness
- ▶ Student Engagement
- ▶ Vocabulary
- ▶ Competency-Based Education

LEARN MORE at MarzanoResources.com/PD